BIG CATS

BIG CATS

Douglas Richardson

WITH ILLUSTRATIONS BY ROSANNE STRACHAN

Whittet Books

(TITLE PAGE ILLUSTRATION) *A composite big cat, showing all the markings of the eight species. Starting with the head: tiger, jaguar, cheetah, clouded leopard, leopard, snow leopard, puma and the tuft of the lion's tail.*

(ENDPAPER ILLUSTRATION) *Jaguar coat pattern* (Ray Charter)

First published 1992
Text © 1992 by Douglas Richardson
Illustrations © 1992 by Rosanne Strachan
Whittet Books, 18 Anley Rd, London W14 0BY
All rights reserved

Design by Richard Kelly

ACKNOWLEDGMENTS

I would like to thank Dr Jo Gipps for suggesting that I should be the one to write this book and to Jo and Leo Laidlaw who gave me a computer with which to write it. My thanks to Dr Andrew Kitchener and Graham Law for their comments on the draft copy. Lastly, my apologies and thanks to Annabel Whittet, a most patient lady.

The author and publisher gratefully acknowledge the permission of the following to reproduce colour photographs on the following pages: Ray Charter p.25 (top two), p.86 (bottom), endpapers; Bruce Coleman p.25 (bottom), p.27, p.28, p.85, p.86 (top), p.103 (top), p.104 (both).

British Library Cataloguing in Publication Data
Richardson, Doug
Big Cats. – (World Wildlife Series)
I. Title II. Strachan, Rosanne
III. Series
599.74

ISBN 0-905483-92-8

Typeset by Litho Link Ltd, Welshpool, Powys, Wales
Printed and bound by South China Printing Co., Hong Kong

(w) 599.744 28 R

Dedication
To my friend, Alison

CONTENTS

Introduction

There are between thirty-five and thirty-eight species of cat depending on which authority you look at. They are loosely split into the big and small cat groups according to some rather questionable characteristics that are supposed to be unique to each division. Small cats are supposed to eat their food in a crouched position, while big cats eat lying down. I have seen all of the big cats eating in a crouched position at one time or another, though small cats seem to bear their half of the behaviour out.

Big cats are supposed to roar and small cats purr. Well, only the lion, tiger, leopard and jaguar can roar. They are able to do this due to the hyoid bones that support the larynx (voice box), having two parallel elastic ligaments in place of the central bones as in the non-roaring cats. The snow leopard is the exception: they have this elastic apparatus, though not as pronounced, but cannot roar. Most cats, large and small, can purr in one way, shape or form, though if they roar, they can only purr when they exhale.

My definition of 'big cats' is purely based on size. I have picked the eight largest species: lion, tiger, leopard, jaguar, cheetah, puma, snow leopard and clouded leopard. All eight species are endangered in parts or all of their range, and each is both a flagship species in its habitat and a popular zoo species with the possible exception of the clouded leopard that is kept by only a few zoos.

Most species of animals can be further divided into subspecies that are physically and geographically distinct and should be treated as separate entities though they can interbreed and produce viable offspring in a zoo situation. The issue of subspecification is a troublesome one for conservationists as many zoos have, usually through ignorance, mixed pure-bred animals of different subspecific status to produce generic examples of the species that bear no genetic resemblance to any wild representative. The importance of whether an animal is pure or not comes when we endeavour to conserve a type in captivity as a safeguard against extinction in the wild or as a possible source of fresh stock for a wild population that has become isolated genetically.

My area of expertise is in the captive management of these living treasures and I have tried to give the reader a clearer idea of how we manage these animals, and more to the point why good zoos are an important part of the conservation community. There is much misinformation about zoos and how they have gone past their sell-by date. Big cats have been kept in captivity for about 3,000 years starting with the animal collections of the ancient Egyptians and the emperors of China. They were kept as curiosities until the 1960s, when a few enlightened institutions began to realize what was happening to the wild and the creatures that lived there.

We are now at the stage, where most zoos are no longer a drain on the wild; rather the reverse. The fact that there are three times as many Siberian tigers in zoos than exist in the wild is testimony to how zoos can manage these species successfully. Reintroduction of captive-bred animals can replenish the wild in many cases. The project with golden lion tamarins in Brazil demonstrates this. The reintroduction of large carnivores is a whole other matter. It may never be possible except in large fenced-off pieces of the wild, but we must keep our options open. It is a new aspect of zoo biology and techniques are being developed that assist us in the race against extinction. For most of the big cats their former ranges either no longer exist or if they have protected areas, these are too small for the remnant populations of cats that exist there to expand. I have included essays on captive management and field observations as I believe that the two are now inextricably linked. If the numbers of a species drop to critical levels we must be prepared to take advantage of all the conservation tools we have at our disposal. Captive management of big cat populations is not the ideal answer, it is but one of the weapons in the conservation community's arsenal. I have worked in zoos for seventeen years, but I'm not interested in living in a world where the only chance I have of coming face-to-face with a tiger is if I open the wrong door.

Douglas Richardson
March 1992

Comparative Big Cats

All the eight species of big cat are near or at the top of the food pyramid in their respective ranges, which puts them in the most precarious of positions in the extinction stakes due to their reliance on finding enough prey animals, which are in turn dependent on dwindling food sources. As with all animals and plants, habitat loss is a severe cause for concern. But, due to their high profile in the eyes of poachers, hunters and farmers it is possible for big cats to disappear long before their habitat does. They are large and dangerous and their body parts are sometimes viewed as being of great medicinal value. The tiger is a walking apothecary according to traditional Chinese medicine.

So, who are the big cats and how do they tick? The coat patterns are the most distinctive features of most of the eight species and it is those characteristic patterns that brought many of them to the brink of extinction. The rosette patterns of the leopard and the jaguar appear similar until you look a little closer. The rosettes of the jaguar tend to have a solid black dot in the centre whereas the leopard's do not. It is easier to look at general build to tell the two apart. The jaguar is built like a weight-lifter, bow-legged and heavily set, and the leopard more like the gymnast in that it is lean but muscular: more definition, less mass. The clouded leopard, as its name implies, has a dark coat made up of large blotchy markings. All three species have a coat marking than can render them invisible in dappled sunlight as it comes through the foliage above them imitating the shadows cast by the leaves of trees.

The snow leopard has grey foggy markings that allow it to blend in with rocky outcrops or the snow on the mountains. The coat is exceptionally thick to withstand the bitter temperatures and the long bushy tail can be wrapped around the body as further insulation.

The tiger's vertical stripes are the most distinctive of all the coat patterns. It is believed that, like the rosettes of the leopard, the tiger's stripes break up the animal's outline when lying in wait in the long grass of South Asia or the woodland scrub of the forests of eastern Russia and China. The cheetah looks every bit the sprinter it has evolved to be. Its coat is yellow with solid black spots. It generally hunts in the open, so the markings probably offer little if any camouflage, but as it is a diurnal hunter the mix of dark and light markings may assist in its ability to heat up quickly in the morning to be ready to hunt, as has been suggested as an explanation for the zebra's stripes. (The light areas ensure that the animal does not heat up too much.)

The remaining two big cats, the puma and the lion, both have a plain brown coat with no markings except in the cubs which have a spotted pattern that fades with maturity but keeps them hidden when they are still too young to stray far from the den. The lion is an inhabitant of both bush and plain, whilst the puma can be found in almost any habitat type in the Americas. It would appear that a tan-coloured coat is maybe the best all-purpose coat colour to have as the historical ranges of these two species were indeed vast.

Big cats are basically land sharks. They have evolved into very efficient hunters and killers capable of dealing with a wide variety of prey from large grazing animals like antelope and deer to catching fish. They are also opportunistic in that, with the exception of the cheetah, they will readily take carrion whether found or stolen from its rightful owner. In general they are solitary hunters that rely on a combination of camouflage, stealth, speed, binocular vision, and an arsenal of weapons to dispatch their quarry.

Coat colour and pattern allow them to blend in with the surrounding environment and so enables the cats to get within killing range. Their ability to lie very still in what would appear to be minimal cover can make them almost invisible at relatively short distances so that even the keen eye of a wary prey animal would glance past the cat. At London Zoo the width of the tiger enclosure is about twenty metres so you would think that the cats would be easy to spot, but when they are lying on the opposite side of the enclosure under the Russian vine that grows over that part of paddock, they can disappear even to those who work with them every day. Like an avid bird-watcher, your eye is trained to pick up certain signals but sometimes when you are checking the animals your eye will glance over one of them and it is not until you look again will you pick up the cat.

The cheetah is exceptional in that it relies on its speed to catch food. Though it has a higher top speed than the various gazelles that make up the bulk of its diet, it has less stamina. A chase lasting more than a quarter of a mile will probably not be successful as the cheetah is in danger of overheating due to its exertions. The wide nostrils of the cheetah ensure that the cat can repay the body's oxygen debt back quickly. In the event of a successful chase this adaptation allows the cheetah to breathe whilst holding the prey in a suffocating bite.

When a potential meal is sighted a cat will go into hunting mode, staying as close to the ground as is possible and inching into position. When moving through the available cover in this way, most of the movement is in the shoulder blades which move up and down with each step forward. It was thought that cats take wind direction into account when closing in on their prey but field studies have shown this not to be the case (at least with lions).

Lying in wait at a waterhole or in the limbs of a tree are hunting methods that require patience but don't expend valuable energy in a stalk and rush that may last an hour with a high chance of failure at the end. The more arboreal leopard and clouded leopard are well suited to the overhead approach as they appear to be equally at home in a tree or on the ground. The tiger, due to its larger size, will lay in wait on the ground for an unsuspecting animal to happen by.

A cat's eyes, like ours, are facing forward giving them good depth perception that goes with binocular vision; they can judge distance accurately when the moment comes to pounce. Although their eyes are adapted to working efficiently at lower light levels, which allows them to hunt at dawn and dusk, there must be some available light and they cannot see in total darkness; probably in a similar fashion to the domestic cat, which we know can operate in ⅙ the amount of light that we need to see well.

The method of dispatching the prey varies with the size of the catch. If it is small then a bite to the head or body will be sufficient to kill it. The combination of the strength of the jaws and the size of the canines is enough to crush the skull or to puncture major organs. With a larger animal, a suffocating bite to the throat or around the muzzle stops the animal from breathing; meanwhile the fore-claws are maintaining a hold and the hind claws may have disembowelled the catch. The lion, due to its more social lifestyle, will hunt co-operatively. Females hunt together: the advantages are that they can attack bigger prey and are more likely to be successful. While one lion is hanging on to the face or throat, others are setting about the tender belly or hindquarters, so if the prey breaks free from the initial captor there are other lions hanging on to it.

A leopard will endeavour to move its catch into a tree out of the reach of other predators that would try and steal the carcass. A solitary lion or tiger would only be concerned with a stronger member of its own species chasing them away from the catch. A jaguar or snow leopard would be in a similar position due to the lack of any larger carnivores within their range. In areas where there are more than one species of big cat, the larger will harass and occasionally prey on the smaller; this will happen between the larger lion and tiger which will harass the leopard and between the jaguar and puma.

Even where territories do overlap, it is very unusual for there to be competition in pursuit of prey. The lion will generally select large plentiful herbivores like zebra and wildebeeste and the tiger goes for gaur and sambar deer. The leopard will prey upon the smaller species available, like Thomson's gazelle in Eastern Africa and langur monkeys in South Asia, though should opportunity present itself, there can be a degree of overlap in what is caught.

The jaguar is unusual in that it is capable of taking down any other species within its range, but the wild diet includes smaller items like turtles which it is able to consume by using its great jaw strength to cave the shell in and so gain access to the contents. It is also an active aquatic hunter, catching and eating fish and the crocodile-like caiman.

Tropical species like the clouded leopard and the Sumatran tiger will breed all year round, whereas those in more temperate climates will show a higher degree of seasonality, like the snow leopard or the Amur tiger, to ensure that the cubs are born after the worst of the winter weather. A female will come on heat every 30–40 days and her scent and vocalizations will attract resident males. Mating can appear to be a very violent process, the male will try and position himself behind and over the female who will crouch on the ground with her hindquarters slightly raised. As the male begins to mate he will hold the scruff of the female between his jaws so as she cannot pull away; both animals will be growling at this time. As the male ejaculates, his grip on the female becomes more firm and the vocalization from both animals intensifies. Soon after, the male will jump back sharply to avoid the female as she lashes out at him. She will not give chase but quickly calms down and rolls on her back; mating will then occur again in a few minutes' time. A heat will last between four and eight days and a female will be mated maybe forty times on each of those days. The big cat's courting and mating ritual is the same as that of the domestic cat.

In general a big cat mother has to rear the cubs on her own, with lions, which live in a pride situation, being the exception. Though a lioness will leave the pride to give birth, she brings the cubs back when they are able to move about pretty well on their own at 3–4 weeks old. When they are integrated into the pride they will suckle off any nursing female. This seemingly altruistic behaviour in lactating lionesses does have a benefit for the individual, as all the females in a pride will be related to one degree or another; assisting with the feeding of cubs that are not necessarily your own but carry some of your genes helps to ensure the survival of those genes. Litter size is usually 2–3, but cheetahs can have 5–6 cubs. Infant mortality and species longevity are two areas where the wild differs dramatically from captivity. In the wild there is no veterinary service or watchful zoo keepers to intervene when there is a problem, and neither should there be. Wild animals on the whole do not die of old age, in fact they are lucky to make it to adulthood. The larger the litter the greater the chance of the cubs dying from starvation or predation. A minimum of 50 per cent mortality rate within the first year is not unusual; if food is scarce through lack of supply or competition, then the female is going to have a hard enough time keeping herself going, without feeding hungry cubs as well.

If cubs do make it through infancy, at eighteen months to two years old they will be independent of their mothers. They will have seen her hunt and at times assisted in the kill, but now they have to apply the knowledge on their own. Prey selection and hunting technique are now crucial to their survival and due to their smaller size and lack of experience they are more prone to having their kill stolen off them. Once they make it to three or four years old they will have built up a wealth of expertise that improves their life expectancy as adults.

Both male and female adults must hold onto a territory so as to assure a constant food supply and available mates. A male tiger's home range will overlap that of two or three females or, in the case of some jaguar studies, the male's range will encompass one female and the periphery of another. To hold a territory successfully the holder must communicate his intentions to other members of his species in the area. This is achieved by a combination of vocalizations (calling) and scent marking. The calling by an animal, be it the roaring of a male lion within his pride or the screaming of a puma, is the equivalent of saying, 'This is my turf, keep your distance.' Calling by a female cat who is on heat will succeed in attracting the male or males in overlapping or adjacent territories.

Smell is probably the most important form of communication and is normally conducted remotely. Spraying urine at points in and around the animal's territory will act to distance other individuals of the same sex or keep the territorial male aware of the reproductive status of the females within his area of control. Scent glands are located on the cheeks, near the anus, between the toes and the base of the spine. When a cat comes across a scent mark it will smell the spot, hold its head up, lift its top lip up and

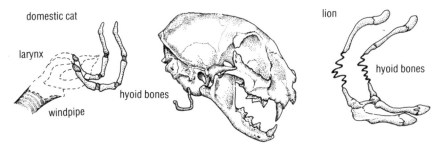

The elastic tissue that connects the lion's hyoid bones allows them to roar. The continuous bone of the domestic cat's hyoid cannot vibrate, hence they cannot roar.

This grimacing tiger is showing Flehmen response in reaction to an interesting smell, drawing the scent through the receptors in the roof of the mouth.

wrinkle its nose as if it has smelt something particularly nasty; this is known as the 'Flehman response'. This action passes the scent through the pair of canals behind the incisors to the vomeronasal organ where the smell is analysed.

The spraying of urine on a tree or rock followed by rubbing on the spot with the cheek or the top of the head enforces the scent on that point in the territory. Faeces are deposited and then scraped with the hind paws as a further advertisement. The covering of faeces by house cats is not usual wild behaviour, where the idea is to make your mark, not hide it. When coming across another cat's scent the finder can tell how recently that location had been marked and, depending on the freshness of the scent, whether it is appropriate to continue in that direction. Though big cats are among the best equipped animals when it comes down to a physical confrontation, for this very reason such a confrontation can have damaging consequences — wounds even to the victor can prove lethal.

Even a less serious injury from a fight with a competitor can reduce your effectiveness as a hunter, the result of which may be starvation. Domestic livestock becomes the only possibility of a decent meal but contact with man will generally result in being poisoned, snared or shot as a pest. Ten to

twelve years would be a good life-span for a big cat in the wild as opposed to 16–20 which is their physiologically possible maximum, which they are only able to reach in captivity.

CITES

These days, at least in Britain, to be seen on the streets wearing a leopard skin coat is social suicide.

In 1973 the Convention on International Trade in Endangered Species (CITES) came into effect. This piece of international legislation controls the movement of animal products among its signatories. The convention divides animals and their products into three categories:

Appendix I species are those that are threatened with extinction and trade can only take place if it poses no threat to the species. Import and export documents are required and these will only be issued in exceptional circumstances.

Appendix II species are those that could be threatened with extinction if trade is not strictly controlled.

Appendix III lists those species that a country protects within its borders and relies on the co-operation of the other states to help enforce this.

All eight big cats are on Appendix I, with the exception of the Siberian tiger, African lion and all but three subspecies of puma. These exceptions to the Appendix I listings are all on Appendix II.

All the large spotted cats were immediately put on Appendix I. There had been a voluntary ban on the use of a number of species, including the leopard, by the International Fur Trade Federation in 1971, but this had been worse than useless as far as the trade was concerned in continental Europe and the Far East. Exact figures are elusive but for the years 1968 and 1969 more than 17,000 leopard skins were imported into the United States alone. Due to the obvious pressure on the species by the fur trade as well as the poison bait campaign that African farmers used to reduce leopard numbers, it was thought that the leopard would disappear if controls were not put in place.

If you allow sustainable use of the animals as a resource for the local people, which is one of the ideas proposed – like for example limited hunting on an organized basis, then the animals have a value to the people of the area and it is in their interests to manage that resource properly. There are still many Westerners who would pay a great deal of money to shoot a leopard. The argument is that the revenue generated by such hunts can directly benefit the community and the perceived value of the animal benefits the species.

One of the problems of such an idea is how to police the scheme: how many customs officials can differentiate between a leopard and a cheetah skin, never mind telling the difference between an African leopard skin and that of the chronically endangered Amur leopard, nor between a legally shot or an illegally shot leopard? And if the controlled shooting of leopard and use of their skins is deemed the most appropriate method of managing the species, then does our revulsion of leopard skin coats lose its meaning?

The lion is the only species of big cat that shows a different characteristic between the sexes (apart from size, which happens in several species): males have manes and females do not.

The Lion

Panthera leo

The lion is probably the best known of the eight species of big cats, the supposed 'king of the jungle'; the trouble with that is that even lions will give way to larger animals like African buffalo or elephants, nor do they live in the jungle.

The lion's present range is mainly confined to conservation areas in the African continent south of the Sahara with the healthiest populations in Kenya, Tanzania, Zimbabwe, Zambia and the Kruger National Park in South Africa. It once occurred in virtually every part of Africa, south-eastern Europe through the Middle East to all of Northern India. The last non-African population is in the Gir Forest in the state of Gujarat, India.

The lion has been divided up into twelve subspecies, though recent evidence indicates that all the African races should be lumped together leaving the Indian (or Asian) lion as the only other variety. They are 2.4–2.9 metres (7.8–9.5 ft) long and will weigh between 120–190kg (265–419 lb).

Lions inhabit open woodland, plains and the peripheral areas of deserts. Their prey are ideally the herds of hoofed animals, antelope and zebra in Africa, deer in India. They are most active at night as it is cooler and though they are thought of as a tropical species, they show discomfort during hot weather. In most temperate zone zoos it is unnecessary to keep them indoors during the winter as they acclimatize well. In fact most zoo lions are many generations removed from their wild-caught ancestors.

Distribution map for lion population.

Are the hyenas waiting for the leftovers, or has the lion just chased them away from their own kill?

Like many carnivores, they are opportunistic hunters and will eat whatever they can catch or scavenge. The spotted hyena has received an unfair reputation as a scavenger. The scene of a lion crouched over the top of a kill surrounded by a pack of hysterical hyenas has been grossly misinterpreted as the lion having to protect its prey. What is more often the case is that the hyenas have made a kill, but they have been chased off the carcass by the larger and stronger lion. The hyena does take leftovers but it is also a very successful pack-hunter in its own right.

A wild lion can eat up to 30 kg (66 lb) at one sitting but then will fast for two or three days. In a zoo an animal will probably need about 2.5 to 5 kg (5.5–11 lb) of food per day to stay fit.

The lion is the only species of cat that consistently lives in social groups called prides. A pride of lions can be made up of two to thirty individuals. All the females in a pride will be related, usually sisters and their daughters and possibly grand-daughters. They are the animals in the group that are responsible for catching all the meals as well as 99 per cent of the parental duties.

The adult male members of a pride are transient and usually number just one male or two brothers. The duties of the males are defending the pride from strange males and getting the females pregnant. Should a new male oust the resident male, the newcomer will kill all the cubs that are still suckling. This sounds rather heartless, but what it does is cause the mothers to come back into heat and so give him the opportunity to pass on his genes to the pride. This type of infanticide has also been documented in other social mammals, namely gorillas and Przewalski's horses. (The average gestation period of a lion is 110 days.)

The mane of the male lion is probably the species' most unique feature. It probably plays two related roles, making the male look more impressive to competitors and giving protection to his throat in a fight. The colour of the mane is always darker than the coat and may even be black and extend right along the animal's belly, though this trait was more commonly found amongst the extinct Barbary or Atlas lion of North Africa which disappeared forever in the 1920s. Some zoos label their lions as Barbary lions, but they are just animals that have been selectively bred to look like this extinct subspecies as they have a smattering of Barbary lion genes from animals that were kept by the monarchy of Morocco.

The lion's roar is both used for keeping in touch with members of the pride and declaring territorial rights so as to minimize conflict with neighbouring prides. The clip of a lion at the beginning of old MGM films is slightly misleading in that the sound is indeed of a lion roaring, but the footage is of a lion growling. When a lion roars the head is held slightly down and the animal has a look of deep concentration on its face.

In the wild, death is likely to be from injury; if a lion breaks a canine it can be susceptible to infection through the tooth or less efficient in catching its prey. Males can be crippled in fights and they all can die of starvation when game is scarce. In other words wild animals do not die of old age. Life in the wild is a constant battle that takes no prisoners.

In a zoo these pressures are removed and so the animal becomes prone to ailments that we associate with old age, like arthritis and kidney disease, that don't get a chance to manifest themselves in the wild.

THE UNKNOWN LION

Most people associate lions only with Africa and yet historically lions occurred from Greece to central India. The last remnant of the Asian or Indian lion occurs only in the Gir Forest in Gujarat in north-west India. As of May 1990 their numbers stood at 284 in a 1,400 square kilometre area that includes the Gir Forest Sanctuary and the surrounding forest plus approximately 70 in zoos.

This is the lion of biblical fame and a prime consumer of Christians in the Roman games. The last recorded sighting outside of India was in 1942 in southern Iran where a single specimen was seen on the Kharki River. The Indian lion differs from the African in having an abdominal skin fold that runs from between the fore-legs to the hind legs. Males have a less prominent mane – the ears and the fore-legs are usually visible.

During the British occupation of India it was fashionable to go on a lion shoot. One officer shot fourteen lions in the Gir in ten days. Due to this hunting pressure the lion became very scarce, and in 1900 it was declared a

This Asian lion has caught and killed a peacock, a prey item that is not on offer to lions in Africa as it is a uniquely Asian species.

protected animal, though in the Gir, the nawab still retained the right for his 'important' guests to shoot a number of animals.

Prior to World War I it is thought that the lion population dropped to less than thirty animals due to a drought that caused the lion's prey to disappear. This number may be an under-estimate due to the nature of the census but it is probably safe to say that they fell to below 100 and as limited hunting was still going on such a low figure would not have been able to withstand any further pressure.

In the early 1980s the captive Indian lion population in Western zoos stood at over 200 animals, so it seemed the future of the subspecies was assured even if the wild population were to disappear. But the captive animals all stemmed from about seven founder animals and it came to light that some of the founders were not of pure origin, namely a pair from the Trivandrum Zoo in India. A study was carried out to look at the genetic make-up of the captive stock. Using individuals of known origin, the genetic structure for both pure Africans and pure Asians was established and then all the captive animals were analysed and compared. Sure enough, all but four or five animals proved to be hybrids and all the work on building up captive numbers had come to naught, as the four or five pure animals were now of pensionable age. The genetic study had also shown that the two varieties of lions have been separated for about 100,000 years. The problem of breeding pure subspecies for re-introduction is one I shall talk about later (see p. 54). Sakkarbaug Zoo, which is very near the Gir Forest, has had a successful breeding programme for pure-bred Indian lions for many years. They usually keep about thirty individuals in the zoo and have supplied

(OPPOSITE, ABOVE) *The most obvious difference between the African (LEFT) and Asian (RIGHT) lion can be seen when you compare the manes of the males. Whereas an African's mane will cover his ears and the top of the forelegs, the Asian's is not nearly as extensive.*

(OPPOSITE, BELOW) *It is often said that female cats carry their young around by the scruff of the neck; in actual fact the mother (in this case a lioness) will grip the cub around the neck, holding it in the gap behind the canines.*

(OVERLEAF) *A leopard is completely at home in a tree, as it climbs quickly and easily. A tree is a safe dining area free of any interruptions. The dappled light through the leaves show the camouflaging effect of the coat pattern which enables the leopard to lie hidden in the tree waiting for a potential meal to wander underneath.*

potential breeding groups to other zoos, mainly in India. Their captive stock is continually augmented by wild caught individuals from the forest that have become injured or that are causing problems to the human population in and around the forest by taking livestock or attacking people.

This problem of lion versus human interests is one that has become more severe in recent years. In the past when drought diminished the numbers of wild prey, cattle, camels and goats were the lion's only option. Recently the number of attacks on people has increased due the growth of the wild lion population and the inability of the sanctuary to contain them. In the last two years there have been some ninety attacks on locals with at least fifteen deaths. The government would like to relocate groups of lions to areas of their former range, but as India has a severe population problem there is every chance that any such moves would meet with strong opposition from the locals; the short history of reintroductions of wild animals into areas they formerly occupied proves that they are doomed to failure without the backing of the people who live in and around the project area.

In 1957 a male and two females were moved to Chandraprabha sanctuary in Uttar Pradesh. They bred and in 1965 the group numbered eleven, but shortly after that no trace of them could be found or reason for their disappearance established. It has been suggested that they had been poisoned or shot by locals.

For the time being, captivity is the only sure option for surplus lions from the forest; in the hope of breeding pure Indian lions, London Zoo received four lions, two males and two females, from Sakkarbaug Zoo in December of 1990. This was the first group to be sent out of Asia in almost 20 years and hopefully this will be followed by other groups to western zoos. The females were born at Sakkarbaug, but the males were brought into captivity as cubs with their mother who was a cattle killer, a better option than a bullet, as the Indian lion population still is critically low.

The census figure of 284 is encouraging since in 1970 only 180 were recorded, but catastrophe is still not far away. With such a small population confined to a limited area, numbers could be decimated by, for example, an epidemic of rabies or feline enteritis or by a breakdown in the level of protection, as when the sanctuary guards went on strike in 1987 and a number of lions were killed. More topically another extended drought could ravage the region and the lions would starve to death along with the other animals and people.

Unlike domestic cats, tigers do not have an aversion to water. Though this one is merely drinking, tigers will seek out pools to lay in during the hottest part of the day.

LIONS AND THE PILL

In the latter half of the nineteenth century, Dublin Zoo was the envy of the world's zoological collections due to its ability to breed, and more importantly rear lions, with what appeared to be assembly-line regularity. The surplus of lions enabled Dublin to either sell them for much needed cash to run the zoo, or swap them for species that were not represented in the collection.

At the time there was much discussion at London Zoo concerning what the keys were to successful reproduction. Bartlett, who was superintendent at the zoo from 1859 to 1897, suggested a dietary solution. The lions had been fed only muscle meat on the bone and not skin, hair or entrails. Lions eat animals, not just meat and so Bartlett changed their diet to include bone meal and whole small animals. If you fed a lion best steak you would cause various vitamin and mineral imbalances. Rickets, though a rather broad term, is one of the ways the problems would manifest themselves.

Crisp, a researcher at the time, attributed the poor breeding record at London to the lack of private cubbing dens for the mothers to be. When a cat is ready to give birth, she wants a dark, dry, quiet place to have her cubs with no interruptions. In fact they were both right: a balanced diet coupled with a secluded cubbing box and you'll soon have more lion cubs than you can shake a stick at.

Everything was fine until the pro-liferation of smaller zoos and safari parks in the 1960s that maintained large numbers of lions. Once these new collections started producing cubs, the market was flooded.

The problem of 'over-production' is not restricted to African lions, but occurs to various degrees with most of the big cats, certain primates (macaques, capuchins and some baboons) and some antelope species. In fact it can happen with any species in captivity; once the formula to repeated successful breeding has been found and is applied by more and more collections, the population can exceed capacity very quickly.

The preferred solution of reintroducing animals to the wild in suitable, secure habitats is not necessary for African lions, as there is still a healthy wild population in much of the continent. Reintroduction is still a relatively young discipline within the field of zoo biology; the techniques needed for such an operation are still being developed. The release of large captive-bred carnivores presents a whole different set of problems, than, say, the reintroduction of a species of arid zone antelope.

The first line of defence in population control in a zoo is to keep the sexes separate. Most cats are considered solitary to some degree so a solitary life is not unnatural – except for the lion. A pride of lions can be anywhere from two to thirty individuals of various ages.

The two methods of birth control

normally used are surgical, the vasectomy, and hormonal, the 'pill'.

A vasectomy for a lion is as simple an operation for the animal as it is for a man, with two differences. Firstly, most lions, no matter how tame, will not allow minor surgery to take place without a general anaesthetic. Secondly, a male lion does not suffer the mental hang-ups that some human males have about the procedure. They don't know what has

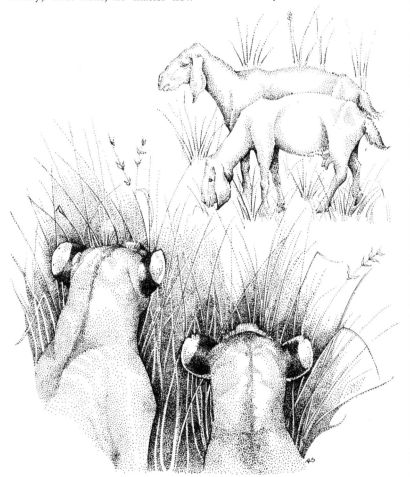

When domestic animals are allowed to graze in wildlife reserves, then some will be taken – in this case by lions. The lions benefit in the short term, but the stockmen will soon persecute the cats to reduce their losses.

happened so they carry on mating regardless, and, as the females don't get pregnant, they continue to cycle and so the male gets the chance to mate more often.

The 'pill', as far as lions are concerned, is a small cylinder about a third the size of a pencil, that is placed just under the skin while the lioness is knocked-out. The site for the implant is usually the inside of a hind leg, and it will remain effective for eighteen months to two years before a replacement is necessary. If breeding is required, then it can be removed and within a few months the female's cycle will return to normal.

It is important that zoos co-operate on a variety of levels when it comes to managing captive populations, and a co-ordinated contraception policy is an integral part of any programme. If there were no communication regarding the use of contraceptive techniques, the population could become destabilized and eventually crash. If a problem is not spotted until too late, then either the animals may be too old to breed or you may be left with sterile males.

There is another method of population control that more closely resembles that of the wild, but that most people find unpalatable. Euthanasia. All the adult animals are allowed to breed unhindered by snipped tubes or hormonal barriers. The females give birth and if a suitable home is not found for the cubs, they are painlessly put to sleep at about two years old.

From the adult lions' point of view, it allows for the expression of natural behaviour: the rearing of young to independence, play behaviour between all the members of the pride including the adult male, letting these animals demonstrate what they have evolved to be. It also avoids the problems of contraception; vasectomies are not as yet reversible, and females who have had implants show a marked increase in the long-term likelihood of tumours of the reproductive tract. Lion cubs in the wild have a tough struggle to adulthood, at best one in five make it to their second birthday. They fall victim to starvation, disease and infanticide.

At the other end of the age scale, most zoos have stopped the rather dubious practice of trying to set longevity records. Most individuals over the age of seventeen probably have a reduced quality of life, and a thorough medical examination would uncover a range of health problems like arthritis, kidney disease and dental problems that cause the animal various degrees of discomfort. As these animals are removed from the population by acts of kindness, more spaces are created for younger animals to allow for a healthy range of ages.

The use of euthanasia as a population management tool seems at first glance heartless. Decisions of this nature are not taken lightly. If you work with an animal every day it is impossible to avoid any emotional bond. If we are going to do what is best for the species and the majority of individuals, then some hard choices have to be made.

The Tiger

Panthera tigris

O f the terrestrial mammals, after the giant panda, the tiger is the most likely species that comes to mind when people think about animals that are endangered. Until well into this century, there were eight different subspecies of tiger, now there are only five and one of those is on the way out. The three extinct subspecies are the Caspian, Javan and the Bali tiger. The living subspecies are the Indian, Indo-chinese, South China or Amoy, Sumatran and the Siberian or Amur tiger.

It took a mere fifty years for the Bali tiger to be declared extinct since it was described scientifically in 1912. Most of the museum specimens were collected during the 1920s and 1930s. By 1960 no sign could be found of the species on the island, though there had been reports of individuals in the 1950s; it is thought that the indigenous population had been wiped out by the end of World War II and that these stragglers were Javan tigers that had swum across the 2.5 kilometre Bali Straits, a distance of no consequence for a tiger.

Tracks of three tigers were found on Java in 1976, but after 1979 no sign of the species could be found.

The demise of these two subspecies is directly related to the growth of the human population and the ensuing need for more cultivated land. In 1815, 12 per cent of Java was farmed and the human population stood at 5 million. By 1975, there were 85 million people and less than 8 per cent of the island was under forest cover.

The Caspian tiger's demise follows a similar pattern to the Javan and Bali forms in that a combination of hunting and loss of habitat to agriculture forced the animals into inappropriate mountain forest areas. It is believed that competition with the more adaptable leopard for the same prey and geographical isolation of the remaining populations were the nails in the tiger's coffin. The last record was of an animal being shot in 1959. It is interesting to note that though the Caspian tiger was harassed by humans into oblivion, there are no accounts of the subspecies resorting to man-eating.

The original range of the tiger was from eastern Turkey through to the north-west regions of China, all the lands south of the Himalayas, and from Siberia south through China, Indo-china to the islands of Sumatra, Java and Bali. Recent studies by geneticists indicate that the species spread out from the area that is the range of the South China subspecies, the most endangered tiger of all, the Amoy tiger. The wild population is estimated at about forty animals with a further forty individuals in Chinese zoos that

(PREVIOUS PAGE) *Recent field studies now corroborate captive observations of tigers as being somewhat more social than was once thought.*

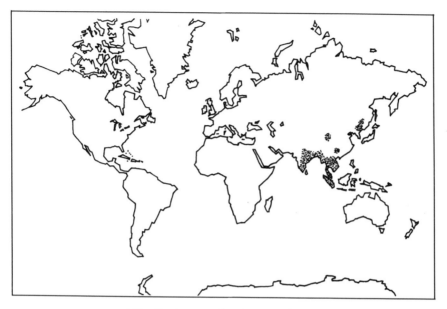

Distribution map for tiger population.

stem from eight wild caught animals. It wasn't until 1977 that laws were passed forbidding the killing of tigers, the need for farmland to feed the most populous country in the world was the priority, and the use of tiger parts in traditional Chinese medicine was an additional pressure. The conservation situation in China is now at the point where the only hope for the subspecies is an organized captive breeding programme.

Tigers are a forest species, hence the striped coat pattern that gives them the camouflage to stalk their prey and get within a few yards before they rush their quarry. Though they will eat anything that they can catch from baby elephants to porcupines, their main prey are the various species of deer and wild pigs as they offer the most return for the energy expended.

The tiger is listed as the largest species of cat, but due to its vast range and the differences in size from a 270 kg (595 lb) Siberian male to a 90 kg (200 lb) Sumatran female, the average for a tiger is about the same as for a lion.

The tiger is not quite the master of his territory as the species of Asian wild dog, called the dhole, which hunts in packs as does the African wild dog, is actively avoided by the tiger. There are authenticated accounts of dholes chasing tigers from kills and a few instances of them killing and eating tiger and leopard.

Tigers communicate through a variety of scent marking and vocalizations.

Female tiger carrying her cub by the neck.

They lead relatively solitary lives with territories that can be from fifty to 4,000 sq. km. depending on prey density. Spraying urine on trees and bushes leaves chemical signals that will warn off territorial invaders or tell a male that a particular female is sexually receptive.

This ability to spray urine backwards for two or three metres does have its comical side in a zoo situation. As the enclosure perimeter marks the extent of the tiger's captive territory, points on the boundary are so sprayed. If that marking location is also an area of fencing that separates the public from the animals and visitors will congregate at the enclosure when the animals are active, the first row of people will be sprinkled with tiger urine when the animal turns its back and lifts its tail. As the first rows jump back belatedly, the back rows move up to the fence to get a better look, but there is normally a second volley and they get an odorous soaking as well.

Tigers have a vast vocal repertoire that extends far beyond their ability to roar. Moans and yowls of both high and low pitches are used. The most surprising of the noises that they can make to people unfamiliar with the species is a vocalization called 'prusten'. It is a friendly greeting that they make to each other or to humans of their aquaintance. The noise is made by expelling air through the nostrils and the mouth in short rapid bursts followed by rubbing heads together with some force. I have been able to copy the call to the point where tigers in my care, and in some instances tigers in other zoos, will respond in kind, though I do draw the line at following the call with a bout of head rubbing.

One of the main differences between managing lions and tigers in zoos is when it comes to rearing cubs. The lion has a long history of successful reproduction in zoos, unlike the tiger. The difference is that a lioness will rear her cubs in a den that is merely out of sight of any human disturbance, whereas only when the mother was given a cubbing den that was also removed from the sounds of humans did the tiger succeed in breeding. The gestation period is about 110 days.

When moving their young about, tigers do not pick the cubs up by the scruff of the neck, but by grabbing the entire neck in their mouths, holding them in the gap behind the mother's canines. This is true of all the big cats.

SIBERIAN MAN-EATERS

When most people think of man-eating tigers, areas like the Sundarbans at the mouth of the Ganges spring to mind with old or injured tigers lying in wait for an unsuspecting human to wander along and make an easy meal. Or they may remember the stories of Jim Corbett, a renowned early conservationist, who would search out a problem animal that had resorted to eating human flesh, and shoot it.

Now the heavily furred giant of the cat family, the Siberian tiger, is causing some concern in the human consumption stakes.

The Soviet population of the Siberian tiger, or more accurately the Amur tiger, formerly occurred from Lake Baikal to the Sea of Japan. Now they are restricted to an area between the Sea of Japan and the Chinese border for about 1,000 kilometres (620 miles) north of Vladivostok. By the 1940s their numbers were estimated at between twenty and thirty. Following the end of World War II, the government banned the killing of tigers and in 1956 limited, then banned for five years, the catching of tigers for zoos.

A number of reserves were established, the most important of these being the Sikhote-Alin in Ussuriland. Thanks to the concerted efforts of the Soviet authorities the number of tigers started to grow. (I've always puzzled over the fact that Russia was a whaling nation when its record for conserving indigenous wildlife was superior to most nations'.)

The Russian researcher, Anatoley Bragin, reported recently that the population may now be as high as 430 animals though there is some doubt whether there are enough prey animals to support this number, hence the conflict with the humans in the area.

Since 1945 there has been a rapid growth in the human population mainly due to the logging industry and the fact that Vladivostok was the base for the Soviet Pacific Fleet. Nikolia Przewalski, the Russian explorer, noted that there were many tigers in the Far East and that they were not afraid of people. With the coming of settlements and armed men, the tigers' behaviour changed and they became wary of people. The implementation of rigorous protection of the animals along with increasing numbers made for bolder individuals and more tigers coming into contact with people and their livestock.

In 1976 a tiger attacked a man in the Lazovsky area. This was the first such attack in fifty years. Another incident took place in 1981, when a cat killed and ate a resident of Terneysky. Since then attacks on humans have become more frequent, though not always fatal. Most of the animals involved in these incidents have been young animals. They would have had no dealings with people and so are not hesitant when it comes to

The lack of adequate prey, coupled with the encroachment of humans into Siberian tiger habitat, can have unpleasant repercussions for both parties.

approaching human habitation to feed on livestock. They are also the individuals that are finding life the hardest as they are too old to stay with their mothers; as well as having to find their own territories, they are still learning how and what to hunt.

Wild boar made up a large proportion of the Amur tiger's diet, but they have all but disappeared from the tiger's range as the hunting and consumption of wild boar is also a favourite human pastime.

This confrontation between large carnivores and humans is one that will continue to hamper conservation efforts. Our ever-increasing population more and more comes into contact with an ever-decreasing wild. How do you convince people that sporadic attacks resulting in loss of livestock or human life are part and parcel of the cost of having wild tigers? Financial compensation schemes only go so far in dealing with the problem. If you live in an area where there are cars, you run the risk of getting run over. Nobody seriously suggests that we abolish traffic, but that precautions are taken to try and avoid the situation arising again. If we are to have large potentially dangerous animals running wild on our planet, we have to find ways to lessen the chance of accidents while creating an awareness of the animal's right to life as well.

SPECIES SURVIVAL PLAN FOR SIBERIAN TIGERS

If we are going to manage captive populations of endangered animals, simply expanding numbers with no thought to long-term implications can lead to disaster. Just such a situation almost arose with the Siberian tiger in zoos.

Starting in the 1960s zoos kept increasing numbers of Siberian tigers due to their availability from the Soviet Union. In many cases they displaced the more commonly kept Indian tiger. As the Siberian is the largest of the subspecies it is a more impressive exhibit. Siberians are no more difficult to breed than any other variety, so a surplus problem began to develop, and soon zoos that originally could not afford to acquire the animals were receiving surplus stock from the larger institutions and so more tigers were produced.

It became virtually impossible to dispose of surplus animals and many collections opted not to breed from their stock at all. Contraception procedures like vasectomy and birth control implants were used along with separation of the sexes to prevent unwanted cubs. A strange situation developed, not uncommon today, where the captive population was large but the wild one was very small and there was no possibility of re-introducing captive animals into the wild as the original habitat was far from safe due to the human pressures on it.

At a meeting of American zoos in 1980, the idea of species survival plans was suggested and adopted by the American Association of Zoological Parks and Aquariums. The species specific plans were to address the problems of long-term management of small populations in zoos that might need to be maintained for a hundred or two hundred years, depending on the state of the wild, which is almost always a depressing projection.

The main problems were reckoned to be preserving genetic variability by avoiding or at least minimizing inbreeding, equalizing the genetic representation of the wild-caught founders so that no wild genes would be lost, and creating a healthy age structure in the captive population.

If you draw one side of a pyramid on a graph with the left half representing males and the right half females, then the horizontal axis represents numbers of animals of a particular age and the vertical axis represents the age of that group, with the youngest at the bottom and the oldest animals at the top of the pyramid; this gives an idea of how a healthy population of animals should look. With the tigers the pyramid was upside-down. Very few zoos were breeding their tigers through choice and so there were not enough young animals being recruited into the zoo population to sustain it for the future.

Some animals were carrying important wild genetic information that looked as though it was going to be lost. What was happening was that zoos were unconsciously selecting their breeding animals according to artificial criteria. If a particular animal proved very aggressive to its selected mates no cubs would be forthcoming and a 'calmer' individual would be used. Domesticity was creeping into the tigers.

Two things needed to be calculated: how many animals were needed to keep the species, or in this case the subspecies, going indefinitely? And was the carrying capacity of the

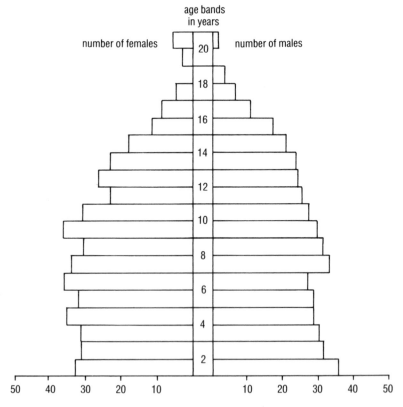

This is an example of a healthy population pyramid, with a broad base of young animals and a narrow peak of older animals. If the pyramid's shape was inverted, with a narrow base that got wider as you went up the age bands, then this would show a low level of breeding (fewer young animals) and a larger ageing population.

zoos involved (in other words the number of cages) sufficient for the number of animals required?

A ten-person committee was elected by the participating zoos to run the Siberian Tiger Species Survival Plan. They would decide who would breed, with whom and when. This dating game can seem straightforward on paper but the practicalities of its implementation can be more of a problem. So it was with George and Martha, two tigers at the Philadelphia Zoo. The Committee had deemed that George should be moved from the Minnesota Zoo in Wisconsin to Philadelphia to mate with Martha. Their progeny would not be inbred and the new match would enhance the goal of preserving genetic diversity. Success in the form of little striped bundles of fur was not to come as quickly as anticipated. For two years Martha would call to George, as female tigers do when they want to mate, but he was not swayed. They finally mated and on February 14th, 1987, two cubs were born later to be called Bira and Lantar.

On the other end of the scale, as animals become reproductively inactive through age and ill-health they still take up cage space that is needed for younger animals that are ready to start producing the next generation. In these cases humane euthanasia is a rational answer. People have difficulty in coming to terms with this, but what has to be borne in mind is that we are trying to save species; sometimes the individual has to be sacrificed for the benefit of the whole.

Detroit Zoo had three such animals that after careful consideration they had decided to put down to make way for younger breeding stock. In 1982 the new director, Steve Graham, had taken the brave stance of discussing the subject of euthanasia of surplus animals with the local media. The general story was followed by a report that was leaked to the press of the decision concerning the tigers. Letters of complaint streamed into his office but most were satisfied when they received a factual explanation for the decision.

One citizen was not so easily persuaded and promptly filed a lawsuit against the zoo for $1 million accusing the zoo of acting in an arbitrary, capricious and malicious manner. A judge issued an injunction to delay action by the zoo until a hearing could be held on the matter.

After six weeks the injunction was removed after a five-hour hearing in which the zoo's case was supported by a large group of professionals from the fields of medicine, dentistry, veterinary science and biology and representatives from other zoos. The postmortem on the three animals proved the zoo's case. The 17-year-old female tiger had a severe kidney problem and the males aged 16 and 11 had serious hip dysplasia. The delay in the procedure by a 'caring' member of the community had caused additional unnecessary suffering to the three tigers as well as delaying the proposed breeding programme.

THE TROUBLE WITH NUMBERS

Project Tiger was the initiative of the Indian Government to save what is regarded as a national, if not an international, living treasure. At the turn of the century, it is estimated that there were possibly as many as 40,000 tigers in India alone. Then, the main pressure on them was hunting by the Indian princes and the ruling British. 'Sport' continued to affect tiger numbers until 1970 when the hunting of tigers was banned in the country.

One of the first tasks of the project was to find out just how many tigers were left in the country. A national census was carried out in 1972, which found a total of 1,827 animals. The following year nine special reserves were established in prime tiger habitat; today there are a total of eighteen Project Tiger reserves.

One of the problems in the establishment of these reserves was the rather heavy handed methods used to relocate people who had been living in the area. There was no real attempt to educate or involve the local people in the project. A similar mistake has not been made in Rwanda, Africa, with the

Competing male tigers will normally try to avoid physical confrontation, but if they are fairly evenly matched, then a fight will follow the circling behaviour as each looks for an opening in the other's defences.

establishment and operation of parks to save the mountain gorilla. The local people here have been involved with the project: there have been educational visits to schools; they have benefited from revenue generated by the tourist trade, and there is a general feeling that this is a part of their lives and they are not treated like ignorant peasants.

To save the tiger whole villages were moved from areas where they had lived for generations, with no consultation. Those that lived on the periphery of the reserves were told that the area of the parks was no longer a resource that they could use for the collection of firewood or grazing for their livestock. This process of alienation, which started during British rule, probably contributed to the reasons for tribal 'terrorists' reclaiming their ancestral land in the Manas Tiger Reserve in Assam. The Manas is considered the richest wildlife region in India and is the second largest of the special tiger reserves. The destruction of the area by the rebels and the poachers that followed will have a long-term effect on the region.

In the Sundarbans of India and Bangladesh between 50–60 people were being killed by tigers each year. It was noted that the vast majority of attacks came from behind. Masks depicting a human face were issued to the locals that frequented tiger country, the masks being worn on the back of the head to fool the cat into thinking that it was being watched. The masks were almost completely successful; those who were attacked had taken their masks off for a moment, so breaking the illusion.

In 1990 the national tiger census listed 4,334 animals which at first glance appears to indicate the success of the project. Valmik Thapar thinks not.

Thapar has been working with the tigers in the Ranthambhor National Park since 1976. He is a well respected expert on the species and its conservation needs in India, and in his informed opinion the actual number is somewhat less than 3,000. In Sariska Tiger Reserve the 1988 figure for the tigers in the area was 44. The following year, after a new field director had been appointed with a knowledge of tigers, the population was reckoned to be 18. In many of the reserves the counts of tigers are carried out by poorly paid, under-educated, badly motivated staff. The edges of the parks are eroded by the locals for much needed firewood and fodder for their animals. In some areas poaching goes on to supply the animal products for traditional Chinese medicine. One of these products is tiger bones.

Due to the recognized importance of the tiger in India a director of a park sees a steady annual increase in his tigers as a ticket to promotion, so any reported tiger sign gets jotted down as another individual, never mind if there aren't enough prey animals in the park to sustain the numbers of tigers reported.

The situation is further exacerbated by the fact that most, if not all, of the reserves have become islands of forest due to the degradation of the surrounding land. The country now has only 8 per cent of its former forest cover, though official figures put it at 13 per cent. The population of India is now at or near the one billion mark. None of the parks has enough tigers for a self-sustaining population and the wooded corridors that once would have allowed for the movement of individuals from one area to another don't exist, so extinction by inbreeding is a real possibility.

Project Tiger, once hailed as a great success, needs to be looked at once again if indeed the Indian tiger is to be declared safe from oblivion.

Like foxes in Britain and racoons in North America, leopards will frequent the gardens of suburban Nairobi in search of food, be it food waste in a rubbish bin or the odd house pet.

The Leopard

Panthera pardus

The leopard has the largest range, west to east, of any species of cat, large or small. Though their populations have become somewhat more fragmented recently, they occur throughout Africa with the exception of the Sahara desert, from the Arabian peninsula up to Turkey and right across the southern half of Asia, north through Eastern China to the land bordering the Amur river. There are two island populations on Sri Lanka and Java. The Javan leopard is peculiar in that though the species extends right down to the tip of the Malaysian peninsula, they skip Sumatra and yet occur on Java. No trace can be found of the leopard ever having lived on Sumatra though the island would have connected Java with the mainland.

The leopard is an extremely adept climber and in areas where they compete with other large carnivores, like lions and tigers, they will drag their kills up into trees and feed unmolested. A leopard can weigh between 25 and 50 kg (55–110 lb); as with all the subspecies and species of big cats the male will be from 10–40 per cent larger than the female, and is capable of pulling a carcass equal in weight to itself up into a tree. The technique used is to hold the prey by the neck with their legs straddled either side of the body, and then shin up the trunk using the fore-claws like ice axes and the hind claws like crampons. Once the body is safely wedged in a fork they can spend two or three days consuming the kill depending on its size. This preference for feeding at height was demonstrated by the Persian leopard, Fritz, at London Zoo. We had a platform built in the enclosure that was about 6 metres from the ground. Once he had investigated the new addition to the cage furniture, he would regularly take his meals to the top of the platform and eat them there rather than in other locations in the enclosure.

There are fifteen subspecies recognized, four of which are managed in zoos by the *Rare Leopards Studbook*. These are the North Chinese, Amur, Sri Lankan and Persian leopards. As with all living things they each have a scientific name that remains pretty constant no matter where you are in the world as 'common' names can differ from area to area. The scientific name is international, and, when you use it, everyone can be clear about what animal or plant you are talking about. The scientific name may be descriptive of the animal concerned, using a physical feature, or it may derive from the discoverer's name, or geographical location. The North China leopard is a prime example of the mistaken use of a geographical location in the name. The North China leopard's scientific name is *Panthera pardus japonensis*. A skin of this subspecies was bought in Japan and the subspecies was described on the strength of that skin. This further misled people into including Japan in the range of the species, whereas like Sumatra, no trace can be found of leopard ever having occupied Japan. The skin was later correctly identified as coming from the North of China, but the rules state

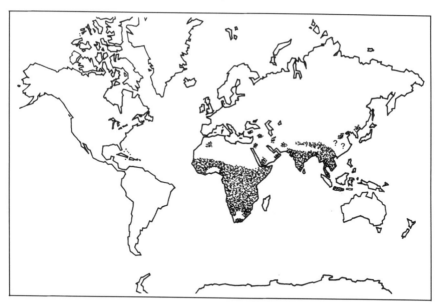

Distribution map for leopard population.

that the first name a subspecies gets, it keeps. So we are left with the Japanese leopard that comes from China.

The pattern of the leopard's coat gives it ideal cover in a tree or hidden in bushes on the ground. The pattern is similar to the jaguar's except that the jaguar generally has a black dot within the rosette markings. This ability to be almost invisible, coupled with its varied list of prey species, has allowed the leopard to hang on in some pretty inhospitable places. The leopards of Sinai live in an arid mountainous region preying on ibex, a type of mountain goat, and hyrax (a small rodent-like distant relative of the elephant). They number about thirty and have been quite closely studied. Due to their prey retiring to cliffs at night, the Sinai subspecies uncharacteristically hunts during the day.

In a similar fashion to the lion, a male leopard has been known to kill a litter of cubs, causing the female to come back into heat, and so allowing his genes to be passed on. Possibly in light of this behaviour, an adult male was seen to guard a cave where there were young cubs, while the female was off hunting. Gestation period for the leopard is about 95 days.

Because the leopard lives its life generally outside the gaze of humans, it was very difficult to ascertain numbers with any accuracy. Surveys that were

done could only indicate that there were leopards in a particular region, they couldn't say how many there were.

The leopard is probably the most adaptable of all the big cats. It is even prone to raiding rubbish bins and stealing poultry and domestic pets in the suburbs of Nairobi. The species can inhabit dense forest, semi-desert, grasslands and mountainous regions.

In the mid 1980s, a new method of collecting a census was used on the leopard. All leopard data from every possible source in Africa was fed into a computer. The data was then plotted over a satellite map of the continent that highlighted the types of vegetation the leopard can be found in. The results gave a population of 600,000 to 900,000 individuals between the Southern border of the Sahara Desert to the Cape of Good Hope. As the leopard is not a species that lives in groups, the figures indicate a very healthy situation for the African leopard at least.

So should the species lose its endangered status?

The Persian leopard's range is Iran, Iraq and Afghanistan. Due to the human conflicts that have plagued this part of the world for some years, the hundred or so animals in captivity take on a more significant role.

Leopards within the range of the giant panda were, for a while, persecuted by Chinese guards employed to protect the panda by the dubious technique of killing one rare animal to protect another, when there was no hard evidence that leopards were significant predators of the panda. Leopards are also supposed to prey on gorillas, but again these accounts are highly suspect and any predation must be exceptional.

In captivity, a leopard is sexually mature at three years old and will live into its late teens. Wild data of this nature is more sketchy due to the animal's low profile.

With the dead gazelle wedged up in the tree, the leopard can consume it at its leisure out of the reach of hyenas.

REINTRODUCTION OF AMUR LEOPARD

The Amur Leopard (*Panthera pardus orientalis*) is the most northerly of the fifteen or so subspecies of leopard. It was formerly found in Korea, Manchuria and throughout eastern Siberia. Once plentiful and even something of a hazard to the humans within its range, the animal's boldness was such that locals used to find pawprints in the snow on the outskirts of Vladivostok. Soviet biologists who have studied the animal believe that there may be as few as 20–30 individuals in the USSR with a smaller number in neighbouring China and North Korea. Most of these animals inhabit the area of the Kedrovaya Pad Nature Reserve which is near the border with China and Korea. So elusive is the leopard that researchers did not succeed in photographing the animal in the wild until 1988.

One of the recommendations of the Russian research team is to augment the small wild population with captive-bred animals. The plan is to train them for a life in the wild and release the young adults in areas adjacent to existing leopard territories so that the captive-bred animals can expand the wild gene pool. From the combined zoo and wild stock some individuals can then be used for relocation to a proposed new and larger reserve in former leopard habitat south of the Sikhote-Alin mountain range. This area is under threat from Korean contract loggers so an alternative site may need to be substituted.

The training that the zoo cats would need is a combination of the art of hunting and a fear of humans. In most zoos it is deemed inappropriate to feed carnivores with live prey nor are they fed with animals that would form their prey in the wild. In fact in the United Kingdom it is illegal to feed a live vertebrate to another animal, never mind the fact that most zoo cats will stalk and catch birds and mice that stray into the cages. So before being released the cats would need to learn what prey is appropriate, like roe and sika deer, and how to catch and kill them quickly.

Captive animals become familiar with humans due to their proximity in zoos. They see the zoo visitors outside the enclosures and relationships can develop with the keepers who work with them every day. The highlight of any tourist safari to East Africa is to see leopard as they are very secretive by nature; captive animals lose this caution of humans and any re-introduction programme of a large carnivore must take into account the possibility of the animal coming into contact with people and the possibly catastrophic results of this contact for the person concerned and the cat.

The Amur leopard is found in the Taiga forests of north-eastern Asia, and has adapted to the severe winter conditions there.

The captive population is no better than the wild one. The zoo population stands at about eighty animals not including a small number in Chinese and Korean zoos. They all descend from nine wild-caught founders and this small sample of the wild gene pool is not evenly distributed throughout the captive population. Seventy-four per cent of the zoo stock stem from just one pair of the original wild founders and one of those animals is of suspect origin. It is believed that the male of this pair may have been from the subspecies that inhabits Nepal (*Panthera pardus pernigra*). This is based mainly on the coat patterns of some of the captive stock. Leopards, like humans, are capable of showing a high degree of individual variation in their appearance, so coat pattern is not an absolute indication of genetic descent.

Such problems of keeping pure genes in small captive populations is not new; the world populations of Père David's deer and the Przewalski horse all descend from 18 and 13 individuals respectively. The herd of 18 deer was collected by the 11th Duke of Bedford and kept at his estate at Woburn. Numbers increased but there was suspicion that a red deer stag had covered some of the Père David hinds. Similarly, there is evidence that the Przewalski horse population carries genes from Mongolian feral ponies that were caught at the turn of the century.

The deer have recently been re-introduced back into China and there are moves afoot to send horses back to their native Mongolia. As both of these species were extinct in the wild, there were no new animals available to be assured of a 'pure' sample to put back in the wild.

There can be difficulties in using impure animals for re-introductions since they may exhibit traits in the wild that are totally unsuitable – for example, they may breed at the wrong time of year. On the other hand, keeping only pure animals of limited numbers can also run the risk of inbreeding. In the case of the Amur leopard, if we accept that this one original male was not of pure stock, are we in a position to be fussy? With the deer and horses there was no choice, and with the critically low numbers of pure and 'hybrid' Amur leopards are we not in a similar boat?

PATTERNS OUT OF THE ORDINARY

I am often asked by visitors to the zoo whether we have a black panther on exhibit. There is a general misconception that 'panthers' are a different species from leopards with their normal rosette coat pattern on a yellow background. In actual fact black leopards are just a colour mutation of 'ordinary' leopards. The name 'panther' does not signify the black version, but is purely a synonym for leopard. In other words you can have a spotted panther or a black leopard and vice versa.

Abnormal coat patterns can be found in all of the big cats, except the snow leopard and the clouded leopard. Which is not to say that those two species cannot show mutation, just that none has yet been documented.

Melanism (black colouring), is fairly common in leopards and jaguar. There have been accounts of black lions, tigers and cheetah, though no specimens exist, as far as I am aware. Black pumas have been collected in Central and South America; all three species occupy a variety of habitats from grassland to dense forest, and it is in the rainforest regions where black leopards and jaguars have mainly been documented. Black jaguars are generally found in the Amazon, though the species' range extends to the US/Mexican border. The black form of the leopard is commonly found in the jungles of South Asia; even though the forests of equatorial Africa are also the home of the species, black African leopards have only been recorded with any regularity in the forests of the Aberdare in Kenya and in southern Ethiopia. This tendency for dark-coated individuals to be found in densely forested regions certainly makes sense if you are a predator. The harder you are to spot, the more chance you have of getting closer to your prey.

For many years there was some debate in zoo circles as to how to get a baby black leopard. Some said that you never get a black cub from spotted parents or that a black pair can produce a spotted cub on occasion. Thanks to the work of Robinson in 1970 and Richard O'Grady, the director of Glasgow Zoo, in 1979, the arguments were laid to rest. They demonstrated that melanism is recessive in the leopard (the opposite of dominant).

As the trait for a spotted coat is dominant over that for a black coat, an individual that carries the genetic codes for both traits will always have a spotted coat. It is therefore possible that an animal with a spotted coat may be carrying a black trait, it just will not show. A black leopard, however, only carries the code for the black pattern, since if it possessed that for a spotted coat, it could not by definition be black itself as the spotted trait will always dominate. The following were found to apply:

1. Pure matings always produce cubs

with the same coat patterns as the parents.

2. If one parent is pure spotted and the other black, for instance, all the cubs will be born with spotted coats but will carry the codes for both traits.

3. If one parent is spotted but carries the black code as well, and the other is black, half of the cubs will be black and the other half will be spotted carriers of the black trait.

4. If both parents are spotted but carry the black gene, 25 per cent of their cubs will be black, 50 per cent will be spotted carriers, and 25 per cent pure spotted.

5. If one parent is a pure spotted animal and the other is a spotted carrier, half will be born pure and the other half will be spotted carriers.

This logic was used for a breeding programme at Glasgow to produce black leopards to order as opposed to chance. They started with a black male and three spotted females that were suspected of carrying the black gene. Sure enough Glasgow soon began to produce a virtual flood of black leopards.

It is commonly thought that black leopards are more aggressive than their spotted cousins, or brothers and sisters if you followed the explanation. O'Grady puts this down to inbreeding, which may be the case in some instances. The belief is self-perpetuating, since if people think black animals are more 'dangerous', they may goad it into springing at the wire. The animal sees people as a negative aspect of its environment and acts accordingly. Two animals which were hand-reared at Howletts Zoo stayed generally friendly to staff.

The breeding of black jaguars does not seem to work in the same way as that for leopards. Marwell Zoo got in a female black jaguar whose parents were both black. She was mated to a male that was as far as was known a pure spotted animal. Her first litter by him consisted of one cub which was black. Her second litter comprised two black cubs and one spotted animal.

Robert Baudy, of the Rare Feline Breeding Center in Florida, has a most comprehensive collection of cats and a breeding record to match. From his experience he believes that melanism, if not a dominant trait in jaguars, operates under a different set of rules than that for leopards. If it was a straightforward dominant gene, then why are there not more black jaguars around? Chessington Zoo has a pair of black jaguars which regularly give birth to mixed black and spotted litters.

The next most famous 'mutant' big cat is the white tiger. This is not a pure albino as it has black or dark

The langur monkey is a prey species for the black leopard in southern Asia, but in this case, as the leopard has caught and killed a porcupine, there is no need for the monkey to escape higher into the trees.

brown stripes and blue eyes. White tigers have been recorded in India for hundreds of years but the first recent live capture was of the male 'Mohan' who was kept by the Maharaja of Rewa at his palace. Mohan was caught in Rewa in May of 1951 and in 1953 he was mated to a normal coloured female who was caught in the same area to begin the white tiger line that we see today.

All the matings from these two animals produced normal patterned coats, and it was not until Mohan was mated back to his daughters that white cubs were produced. A number of these cubs were sent to other zoos including a white female and a carrier male to the National Zoo in Washington DC in 1960, and a pair of white animals to Bristol Zoo in 1963.

Due to the high levels of inbreeding and their subsequent crossing with tigers of non-Indian origin, white tigers have become something of a problem. To purists, they take up valuable cage space that could be used for pure-bred Amur or Sumatran tigers. To realists, they represent a source of revenue for the zoo from their sale or loan to other collections that see them as a money spinner. A proportion of the public wishes to see white tigers, and the money that the animals generate can be used to finance more laudable projects. These animals are produced by the same genetic rules that govern the incidence of black leopards.

Still on the colour white, at the British Museum of Natural History's annexe at Tring, they have a white puma on display. Due to the rarity of such a specimen, I imagine that it may be the same animal that London Zoo bought from the animal dealer Jamrach. The animal arrived at the zoo on May 27th, 1848, until it died there on January 29th, 1852.

On May 6th, 1978, a pair of white leopard cubs were born to a normal pair at the Rome Zoo. Both had to be hand-reared. The male cub was whitish with light grey spots. He died shortly afterwards and the post mortem showed internal abnormalities were the cause of his death. The female cub survived and she was snow white in colour. As she got older, her coat turned pale grey and the spots became visible.

In 1960 two white lion cubs were seen in the Kruger National Park, South Africa. In October 1975, two white lion cubs were born to a normal female in the Timbavati Nature Reserve which is adjacent to the Kruger Park. In August of 1976 a further white cub was born to a different female in a neighbouring pride. There are now two examples of white lions at Pretoria Zoo in South Africa taken from the Timbavati prides. The two cubs born in 1975 were taken into captivity in Pretoria Zoo, where they still are, after the cub born in 1976 disappeared following offers of four-figure sums for a white lion skin. All of these examples of aberrant coat patterns discussed in this section represent the sum of what is known from the wild and zoos.

These white lions, like the white

tigers, are not pure albinos. Their coats are indeed white and their noses and paw pads are pink, but their eyes are yellow. It would appear from the data available that there has been the occasional white cub born in the area for some years. It should come as no surprise that these unusual lions have not been seen as adults; infant mortality amongst lion cubs is very high anyway, and white colouring must be a disadvantage since lions as hunters rely on their colour to blend in with their surroundings. Also, the breeding male of a pride will be ousted by a stronger outsider every couple of years, so if it is a recessive gene that produces white lions, it may take some time for a descendant of the pride that carries the gene to mate with a female relative and produce white cubs.

The last of the unusual forms of big cats detailed here is the king cheetah. Instead of having the even-spot pattern of the species, the spots are much larger, forming three continuous stripes along the back of the animal, the tail is striped and ringed, and the hair is longer with a thick ruff on the neck.

The animal was first described to science by Reginald Pocock of the Natural History Museum, London, in 1927. He was an eminent cat taxonomist of his day. Pocock gave the animal species status and named it *Acinonyx rex*, the king cheetah. He later retracted his decision in 1939 due to the lack of further evidence; a patterned coat does not a new species make.

In Bottriell's book *King Cheetah*, which charts her search for living evidence of this cat, she documents twenty-two skins found between 1926 and 1974. The living animal has been sighted as recently as 1986 in the Kruger National Park after a gap of seven years.

In May of 1981, two sisters gave birth at the De Wildt Cheetah Breeding Centre and in each of their litters there was one king cheetah. Both of the females had been mated by the same male who was wild caught in an area of the Transvaal where king cheetahs had been sighted. Further births have taken place at the centre resulting in more examples of the form.

It would appear from the evidence, especially the captive births, that the king cheetah is to the 'ordinary' cheetah what the white tiger is to the Indian tiger, just another mutation, albeit an interesting one, and not a new species or subspecies. Again, both the trait for the white lion and for the king cheetah is a recessive one, as with the black leopard (see p. 55).

Jaguars are the ultimate big cat opportunists and have been seen actively 'fishing'.

The Jaguar

Panthera onca

The jaguar is the third largest of the world's cats, and the largest in the Americas. It can get up to 2.4 metres (7.8 ft) long and weigh 120 kg (265 lb).

Eight subspecies have been described in a range that encompasses Mexico, through Central America, and as far south as the north of Argentina. The species has probably become extinct in Uruguay, El Salvador, Nicaragua and the United States. It occurred throughout the American south-west well into this century. In 1885, jaguar were spotted north of Los Angeles. In Bolivia, Argentina, Honduras, Panama and Costa Rica the jaguar is considered endangered, and vulnerable in the rest of its range.

When cattle ranching first came to the home of the jaguar, there is some evidence that local populations increased as the jaguar had a plentiful supply of large prey that matched their size and capabilities for the first time (there is no large natural prey left in their habitat). This increase, if it did indeed happen, was shortlived, due to the pressure applied by the ranchers when they saw some of their profits going down the throats of *el tigre*.

A comparison is often drawn between the leopard and the jaguar, probably based on the similar markings (as we saw in the comparisons of big cats, the jaguar has dark rosettes with black dots in the centre). It is more appropriate for the comparison to be drawn between the jaguar and the tiger: the habitat type preferred by jaguars is fairly dense cover near a water course; they take a variety of prey from caiman (a South American crocodilian), to capybara (a giant guinea pig) and tapirs, but generally their prey is smaller as there aren't the herds of larger mammals that the tiger has to choose from. The jaguar is certainly capable of taking large prey, as they are prone to killing adult horses and dragging them off into cover. Their arboreal activities are nowhere near as good as the leopard's; they can climb trees, but most of their activity is based on the ground.

The jaguar's build is like that of a weight-lifter. It has very powerful forequarters supported on slightly bowed fore-legs. In a captive situation, it is treated with more respect than the other cats due to its power and temperament. In my experience, I have never known a jaguar that you could class as 'friendly'. They seem to wait for you to open the wrong door or stand too close to the fence so that they can get hold of you. They do well in captivity with a good breeding record, but there's a sinister undertone that they want to rip your head off. In this way they differ from the other big cats. Leaving aside the acceptability of circuses, it is interesting to note that you very rarely see jaguars in the circus ring. Is it their relative lack of agility or are they also recognized by the circus fraternity as being excessively aggressive compared to the other usual circus cats?

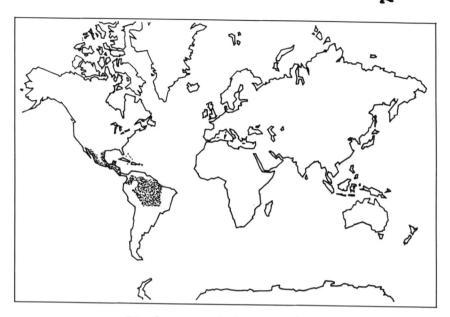

Distribution map for jaguar population.

Their roar is more a repeated grunting cough that you most often hear when there is a female on heat in the vicinity. In the wild she may be followed by a number of males, though only the most powerful will probably do the mating. After around 100 days she will give birth to a litter of two cubs, though this number may vary.

The jaguar has been persecuted throughout its range, though there are almost no accounts of attacks on humans. The skin trade has taken its toll of the species. In 1968, the United States imported nearly 14,000 pelts alone. The introduction of national and international conservation legislation has certainly reduced the pressure on the species, but the killing of jaguars for their skins still continues in many countries due to the protection existing on paper but not in practice.

It is likely that as more reserves are established for the jaguar it will be deemed safe, for a while. But as has happened with similar conservation initiatives concerning the other big cats, when the buffer zones surrounding the parks disappear, so the overflow of animals that are a consequence of a good reserve will venture out in search of food and mates. They will come into contact with human habitation and the killing of jaguar will start again.

ERNIE

Many people believe that zoos still acquire most of the animals that are on show from animal dealers or private expeditions whose express purpose is to catch wild creatures and bring them back kicking and screaming to a life in captivity. Nothing could be further from the truth. When I am taking people round the cat section at London Zoo they are almost always surprised to hear that every animal on the section was either born at London or some other zoo. Just such an animal is Ernie.

Ernie is a jaguar who was born at London on May 13th, 1987, and he is probably fifth or sixth generation captive-bred. His parents were Igor, a male born at Marwell Zoo, and Baby, a female born at Whipsnade Zoo.

In 1975, the New Lion Terraces were nearing completion at London and one of the seven species that the zoo planned to concentrate on was jaguars. They brought in a young pair to start a new London lineage, Igor and a female from Cologne called Margaret. When they matured mating took place on a regular basis, about every 40–50 days which is the normal cycle for jaguars. Unfortunately no little furry spotted bundles were forthcoming so Baby was brought in from Whipsnade to rectify the situation.

It would appear that the problem lay with Margaret because on March 30th, 1983, Baby produced her first litter of cubs. The problem with Margaret was later confirmed when an examination showed that she had ovarian cysts.

Anyway, back to Ernie's story. On January 19th, 1987, Baby showed signs of coming on heat. This manifests itself with the female rolling about on her back, reduced appetite, increased vocalization, and of course the male in the vicinity taking a greater than usual interest in her activities. Basically the signs are the same as you would find in a domestic cat. All this was confirmed by Igor and Baby mating from January 20th to 30th. On each of those days they would mate between ten and twenty times.

Almost as important as a nutritionally sound diet for a mother-to-be jaguar is the need for privacy when the birth comes along. To this end Baby was given nightly access to the cubbing dens on April 20th. These dens are in an area of the building away from the other jaguar night cages so as to avoid Baby being disturbed by other animals in the building and to give her more privacy from keeper activities. The birth was still some way off, but introducing changes to the animal's routine too close to the time is not advisable.

She was still running with the other two jaguars during the day and on April 26th, Igor was seen to make a half-hearted attempt at mating her. Cats, unlike humans, generally only mate when the chemical signals from the female are right. This mating during the last stages of pregnancy has been seen in other cat species, and may be triggered by the hormonal changes in the female.

On April 29th, it was decided to keep Baby indoors due to the impending birth and allow her to settle into a solitary routine with no disturbances from man or beast. The cubbing dens are divided into two areas, one is small, dark and warm with a thick straw bed. This area is inviolate and no keeper should enter this den so the only smell is that of the mother as this is where she will give birth to the cubs. The other area is where the female will be fed and watered. The walls of both these dens are solid with a small wire hatch in the feeding den through which to pass food in and a hole in the wall above the water trough so that it can be kept topped-up. This arrangement allows both operations to be carried out without opening doors and disturbing the female and cubs. The small den has no natural light but the large den has a skylight to allow a natural light cycle as the switching on and off of lights can be a disturbance in itself.

On May 3rd the cubbing dens were cleaned out for the last time. They have a toilet area that they use and so keep the rest of their space faeces-free. From now on Baby would be fed, watered when necessary, and generally forgotten about.

On May 13th a cub or cubs were born. The birth date was 103 days after the last day of mating and was within the normal range of gestation for the species which is anywhere between 97–110 days. This was the female's sixth litter. We did not see them as this would disturb the mother, but we heard the high-pitched squeaking of young jaguars. Other signs are the female not coming over for her meat when it is put in and then only consuming it when nobody is about.

Over the next few days Baby kept a very low profile, but as long as her food disappeared and she remained invisible, it was a safe bet that she was caring for the cubs. After a couple of weeks Baby was coming out for her food as it was put in and as no sounds had been heard from the den, it was decided to shut the dividing door and have a look. We found a very well fed cub sound asleep in the small den.

On June 13th the big den was cleaned out for the first time. Even though it had been six weeks since the area had been cleaned, all the mess was in one corner. On July 11th the mother and cub were given access to the indoor area that connects all the jaguar dens so as to get used to us and the smell of the other animals while they were in the outside enclosure. On the next day mother and cub were moved over to a large indoor cage that had direct access to the outside enclosure, and, while Margaret was indoors, and Igor was up at the zoo hospital having a chronic infection of his paws dealt with, Ernie made his debut in the outside world. The enclosure contains a pool which we drained and

When Ernie the jaguar was first let out into the enclosure at London Zoo, he stayed very close to his mother Baby, as all the sights and sounds were new to him.

padded out with straw as the cub would walk in a straight line right over the edge of the pool. Ramps out of the pool were made out of tree branches as he was too small to jump out. As Margaret would view the cub as something edible, use of the outside cage was on a rotational basis with Baby and Ernie using it in the afternoon and Margaret in the morning.

The next major event in Ernie's life was his first inoculation. Cats, large and small, wild and domestic, are prone to the same diseases. As you would take your house cat along to the vet for his inoculation against feline enteritis, we routinely inoculate the cats at the zoo, first at about 8–9 weeks old and thereafter every year. With cubs you can hold them by the scruff, but with the adults we use a squeeze cage that connects the indoor cages to the outside enclosure. The animals are used to passing through this cage every day so that when it comes time to give them their injection, it is a minimal stress situation for the animal.

It was about this time that we decided upon his name. Ernie was chosen as it was the name of my predecessor, Ernie Swain. Ernie had been the headkeeper of the cats before me and had retired in 1986 after some forty years at the zoo.

On November 14th, Baby was seen to be treating the cub a bit roughly, though at that point it was nothing to worry about as cubs at this stage play quite roughly and sometimes mum just wants to be left alone. On December 16th, his face was swollen on the right side. The next day we knocked him out briefly in order to lance the abscess. On the 18th he was eating again. The injury was probably caused by a claw from his mother, so at this point they were housed separately at night for their food. On February 24th, 1988, Baby appeared to come on heat, so her aggression towards him may have been explained by her gradual return to sexual receptivity. In the wild, the breaking of the mother/cub bond is a gradual process, and this was what we were seeing.

Early in 1989 it was decided to permanently separate Ernie from his mother, not because of fighting, but because he was becoming sexually mature and we did not want him getting his mother pregnant for obvious reasons. Ernie continued as a solitary animal until September 24th, 1990, when he was sent to Cricket St Thomas Wildlife Park to be paired with their female. The introduction went without incident and he has settled in at that country zoo.

Ernie's story is typical of most zoo cats and demonstrates the level to which zoos have become self-sufficient in many species. In 1987 the *International Zoo Yearbook* listed eighty-two jaguars as having been born in captivity. There is absolutely no need for further jaguars to be brought from the wild to augment captive numbers as zoo jaguars appear to be on a sound footing. It is questionable whether the bulk of the wild jaguars are in a similarly secure situation.

THE INCONGRUOUS JAGUAR

All of the big cats, except the cheetah and clouded leopard, are classed as potential mankillers. There is a body of evidence to back this up for five of the species; the jaguar is labelled as such but there is less evidence. Melanie Watt of the University of Toronto's zoology department is carrying out extensive field work on the jaguar in Belize. Melanie has been tracked by jaguars in the reserve area without having been attacked. Part of the tracking process is to follow jaguar prints along trails; on one occasion when she was following tracks it became apparent that the cat had doubled back and was following her at a short distance. Although she must have presented an overwhelmingly tempting target when bending over to measure a print for identification nothing happened.

There are no authenticated reports of jaguars attacking humans, though they are large and powerful enough to do so.

Melanie set about quizzing the local inhabitants about jaguar attacks of which there were allegedly many: some instances where jaguars had supposedly killed cattle turned out to have been manufactured as an excuse for killing a cat. One surprising story was of two Indian children playing at the foot of a tree whilst a wild jaguar lounged overhead just watching the children play and not coiled up ready to pounce. A small human crouched beneath any other predator would have solicited an unpleasant response.

In ancient Mayan culture the jaguar figures heavily in artefacts, not as a fierce killer but in a peaceful pose. Like the tiger, the jaguar is the super-predator in its environment, other than man it has no equals. The jaguar has very catholic tastes in its diet, so why draw the line at man?

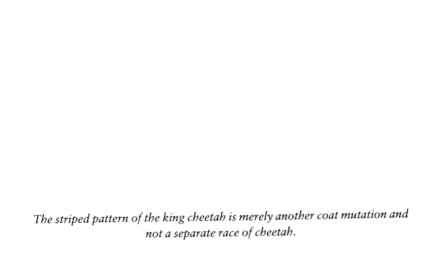

The striped pattern of the king cheetah is merely another coat mutation and not a separate race of cheetah.

The Cheetah

Acinonyx jubatus

The cheetah is most famous for its speed! 115 km (70 miles) per hour has been documented for very short distances, but 80 km (50 miles) per hour is more the norm in a chase. Cheetahs will stalk prey, usually gazelles, but also will amble up to a herd and pick an individual as a target. When the herd starts to run the cheetah begins the chase, getting up to speed in about two seconds. They use their long tails as counterbalances when making sharp turns to stay with their quarry. If the prey does not run, but stands and faces the cheetah, the cat will not follow through. They need the fleeing animal to trigger off the killing response. The mass murder of domestic animals by predators illustrates the same point. If a fox enters a pen containing a flock of chickens, the chickens panic and the killing begins. But, because of the fencing, the rest of the chickens cannot escape and continue to fly about in the confined area, so the fox is constantly presented with the stimulus that makes it kill. The way a domestic cat will take little notice of a piece of string until it is dragged across the floor, illustrates how movement is the stimulus. George III had a cheetah that he set upon a stag, but instead of running from the cat, the deer turned and tossed the animal into the air with its antlers. The cheetah would have nothing further to do with this particularly bolshy deer. The event was recorded in a painting by Stubbs.

Though the cheetah can attain high speed, it cannot sustain it for more than a few hundred yards. After a hard chase it can be near exhaustion and unable to move, protect or eat its catch. Cheetahs, though having a high success rate, will often lose their kill to other carnivores like lion, leopard, hyena and hunting dogs. All four species will also kill cheetahs and their young.

The cheetah is often quoted as having non-retractile claws. This is not true. Most cats have sheaths of skin that the claws retract back into when not in use. The cheetah has no such modification, so the claws are always

A cheetah's dew claw helps to bowl the prey over to allow the cat to gain a throat hold.

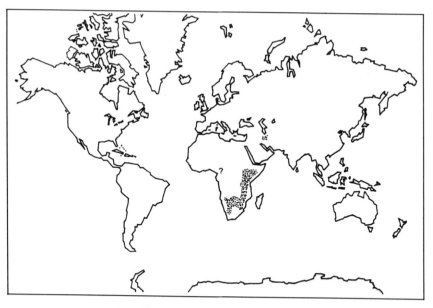

Distribution map for cheetah population.

visible, although they can still be retracted. The equivalent of the thumb, the dew claw on the animal's wrist, is used when it gets close to its prey. The cat will side-swipe the prey with a fore-leg and hook it with the dew claw causing the animal to tumble over; the cheetah is then able to grab the throat and suffocate the creature as its jaws are not strong enough to give a crushing bite. When cheetahs were used for hunting, if an animal had a blunt dew claw, it was not as successful at bringing down the animal it was set against according to hunting records of Indian nobles.

The preferred prey animals are gazelle with a weight limit of about 60 kg (130 lb). Cheetahs begin to consume their catch as soon as they have recovered from the chase. They rarely, if ever, return to a kill and appear not to take carrion. This finicky behaviour when it comes to food has made the cheetah immune to poisoned bait left by farmers, but has not protected it from the farmer's bullet as cheetahs are diurnal and tend to frequent open ground with only limited cover.

The species was once found throughout all of Africa, the Middle East, and from Turkey east across to India. They are now confined to east and southern Africa, and possibly Iran.

Cheetahs give birth to fairly large litters of between three and six cubs after a gestation of about 93 days. The cub's head and back is a dirty white

The cheetah cub's coat mimics that of the ratel, a very aggressive type of badger, and so may offer the cub some protection from predators.

colour. This is believed to give it protection as the marking is similar to the ratel or African honey badger. These animals are about the size of a European badger, but ten times as fierce. I once saw a ratel that had escaped from its zoo enclosure climb a fence into a pen containing a pair of adult Siberian tigers. The cats kept a polite distance at first until the ratel entered the small wooden den in the middle of the enclosure. The male tiger went straight in after it. Right away there was much commotion from within the den and, though I'd heard much of the ratel's reputation, I expected to have to remove the badger's remains.

After about fifteen seconds of growling, etc., the tiger came shooting out of the den with blood coming from a bite on a hind leg. The badger followed it out without a scratch. Both tigers ran into a holding cage next door to escape the small terror. If the coat colour of the cheetah cubs is for protection, then evolution picked the right pattern.

Cheetahs will make use of high points in their territory as lookout posts. These are marked with faeces by the females and urine by the males. A female cheetah of my acquaintance would climb a tree in her enclosure and sit out on a limb over the top of the Brazilian tapirs in the adjacent enclosure. This caused me some concern, but as she had been doing it for a while and never tried to venture down for what would have been prey for a jaguar, it was decided to leave things as they were.

Cheetahs can be found in a number of small groups of different combinations of individuals, except adult females who do not tolerate each other. Groups of males, usually litter mates, will attack single males within their home range. An adult animal will be about 2.5 metres (8 ft) long and weigh around 60 kilos (130 lb). Their captive lifespan is around fifteen years, though less in the wild.

Cheetah calls (what zoologists call vocalizations) are a combination of bird-like chirps, short meows and purrs. When threatening, they will bluff charge, stopping short of their objective and simultaneously stamp both fore-paws on the ground and emit a cough-like spit.

FAMILIARITY DOESN'T BREED

In the latter part of the 16th century the cheetah bred for the first time in a captive situation. The next time the species was to give birth in captivity was in 1956 at the Philadelphia Zoo. Why the large gap between births? The majority of big cats breed fairly regularly, in fact some reproduce far too readily in zoos to the point where contraception has to be used.

Akbar the Great was the 16th century ruler of what is now India and Afghanistan. For hundreds of years the rich and famous had kept cheetahs as hunting animals, setting them after gazelle and hares like spotted lurchers. Akbar kept around 1,000 cheetahs and apparently was keen to try to breed them, even giving them free range of the palace grounds. He was to succeed only once. Many modern-day zoos have not done much better. A number have bred cheetahs, but only once or twice, and

Until fairly recently, the cheetah was used as a hunting animal by humans. The blindfold would be removed once the intended quarry – usually gazelle or hare – had been sighted by the handler.

then failed. Two examples are Philadelphia and Port Lympne in Kent. Both are reputable collections with a will to do the best by their animals, but consistent success has evaded them both.

Places that have regular births like Whipsnade who first bred the species in 1967 and haven't looked back, and Pretoria Zoo's cheetah breeding centre at De Wildt that was set up in 1971 and has been producing home-bred animals since 1975, have observed that if you keep a pair of cheetahs together for an extended period of time and no mating occurs, then it probably never will. When you introduce a pair there should be a period where the male will harass the female and mating then occurs. If they appear to lose interest in each other or at best the romance rapidly begins to resemble that of a human couple of long standing where the sparkle has long since faded, then they should be separated, ideally to cages some distance from each other and another combination of animals should be tried.

Sometimes even this does not work. Graham Law at Glasgow Zoo had been trying to breed the species for some years. He would regularly separate his animals to opposite ends of the zoo and after varying periods of time re-introduce them to each other in the hope that absence would make the glands grow fonder. Early in 1990 one of his females was showing signs of a possible pregnancy, and though nothing was definite, Graham prudently arranged

for Edinburgh zoo to take his other female and so give the remaining female more space and privacy.

As luck would have it his female turned out not to be pregnant but the animal that went to Edinburgh was promptly mated by their male and gave birth to the first cheetahs to be born in Scotland. Graham's actions did indeed produce results, though not quite in the way intended.

The infrequency of cheetah births in the world's zoos has given rise to two schools of thought as to the cause and possible solution:

Camp one sees it as an animal management problem. The lack of matings and the high infant mortality rate in captivity all indicate that it is the humans in the equation that are the root cause of the lack of success. The cheetah is a more complicated animal to deal with in captivity when it comes to reproduction. If more collections addressed the need to move animals more often between zoos when no births have been forthcoming from the resident animals then I think there would be more matings, as has been demonstrated in this country.

The problem of the large number of infant deaths is probably down to the lack of privacy for the female and her cubs just prior to and for a few weeks following the birth. It is still commonly quoted in a number of zoo texts that a first-time carnivore mother will probably abandon or kill her first litter as this is part of the process in her learning to be a good mother. I believe that the reason for this boils down to one of two things. One is that people are unaware that the female is pregnant, so cleaning operations carry on as normal and she still runs with other animals. When the birth comes no cubbing den is made available to her or if there is a dark quiet area, the keeper tries to move her for cleaning and feeding and so disturbs her. The second possibility is that the zoo is aware that she is pregnant but because it is her first litter they keep too close an eye on her and deprive her of the necessary privacy.

Camp two blames the animals. Genetic analysis has shown that all cheetahs are virtually identical so that any matings that do occur are going to produce the same problems that you get from breeding animals that are closely related to each other, brother-sister matings for example. At some point in the dim and distant past, the species went through a genetic bottleneck. Their numbers dropped to very low levels and so the existing animals are inbred. This, they say, accounts for the high degree of malformed sperm in the males and females supposedly not coming into heat.

If this were true then the genes that would cause these problems would have led to their extinction a long time ago. If a population does drop to a small number of individuals, then the deleterious genes are either bred out of the animals or the species disappears.

Camp two suggests that we collect sperm and eggs from all the captive animals, sort out the 'healthy' ones and use artificial breeding techniques like in vitro fertilization, test tube cheetahs, to save this endangered species. New breeding technology can be very useful, but in the case of the cheetah, good animal husbandry has been shown to work and this must be preferable to resorting to the 'test tube'.

A TASTE OF EXTINCTION

The cheetah, like the lion, is generally thought of as a typically African animal. But, like the lion, an Asian subspecies also occurred throughout the Middle East, southern Russia, Afghanistan, and down into central India. Alas, the record of its disappearance from most of its former range makes depressing reading.

In Jordan and Kuwait it was last sighted in 1949. In Arabia the last record was of four animals that were shot by oil workers in 1950. Frank Finn wrote in 1929 that Indian princes were still using cheetahs for hunting, but that they were all imported from Africa. The cheetah was declared officially extinct in India in 1952. Soviet biologists consider it very unlikely that they still hang on in Turkmenia and a programme to introduce African cheetahs into a reserve in Kazakhstan is underway. The Asian cheetah is supposed to be a slightly larger animal with a lighter coloured but thicker coat and a more prominent neck ruff than the African cheetah.

What appears to be the only hope for the Asian variety is the chance that a number still survive in Iran, specifically the Khosh-Yeilagh Wildlife Reserve in north-west Iran. In the early to mid-'seventies, sightings of females with cubs were fairly regularly made by representatives of Iran's Department of the Environment. In the early 'seventies there were also sporadic sightings on the Mooteh Wildlife Reserve in eastern Iran and the Bahram-e-Gour Protected Area in the south of the country. The deposed Shah of Iran may not have been Allah's gift to the man on the street, but during his reign the country did have a sound conservation policy for its indigenous wildlife. After the revolution most of this work came to a halt. It was further hindered by the extended war with Iraq

A project is now proceeding under the guidance of Mohamond Kamir, of Tehran University, to determine the status of the cheetahs in the area of the Kosh-Yeilagh Wildlife Reserve.

Large carnivores are obviously dependent for their survival on an adequate prey base. Recent studies on the African cheetah have shown that in some areas they are almost totally reliant on the population of Thomson's gazelle. Early observations on Indian cheetahs seemed to indicate that their main prey was the blackbuck antelope which is similar in size to Thomson's gazelle; but the numbers of blackbuck have been severely reduced through hunting and habitat loss. For example, there are more blackbuck on game ranches in Texas than in all of Pakistan and American stock has been sent back to Asia for re-introduction. It is then possible that the disappearance of most of the blackbuck herds, along with hunting, spelled the demise of the cheetah in India. Similarly, the disappearance of most of the gazelles on the

Arabian peninsula could have been the underlying cause for the extinction of cheetah there, with the added effect of hunting.

In Khosh-Yeilagh the main prey of the cheetah was the wild sheep of the area. If they have gone then the cheetah cannot be far behind.

It has been said that nothing is ever extinct, it just hasn't been seen for a long time. The Javan rhino is a case in point. For years the only known locality of Javan rhino was the Udjong Kulon reserve on the western tip of Java. The species was formerly found throughout southern Asia. Then, a couple of years ago, a small group was sighted in Vietnam, of all places. Who would have thought that an animal as large as the Javan rhino could have escaped detection, never mind survived, in an area that has been as unpleasantly busy as Vietnam? But then, maybe because of diet, herbivores have the short-term advantage over carnivores in the extinction game.

The expansion of the white-tailed deer population in western Canada has created one of the few recent cases of a big cat's range increasing – in this case the puma's.

The Puma

Felis concolor

The puma is probably known by more names than any of the other cats. Cougar, catamount, mountain lion, American lion, and panther (used for the puma and the leopard) are just some of the English names used, hence the importance of a universal scientific name.

The species once had the largest distribution of any terrestrial mammal in the Americas, from the Yukon to the southern tip of Chile and from the Atlantic to the Pacific coasts. Nowadays, they are all but extinct east of the Mississippi River with two small populations in Southern Florida and the Canadian province of New Brunswick. Curiously, there has been one case of expansion. The British Columbian subspecies has expanded into Manitoba following the white-tailed deer that have moved into that area. By the same token, the deer population in the eastern United States is larger than it was before the American Revolution but there are no pumas left to take advantage of the resource, having been shot, trapped and poisoned out.

A total of twenty-nine subspecies have been described, though, as with the lion there are some questions as to the validity of most of them, particularly those from South and Central America, as they have not been as extensively studied as the North American varieties.

The puma is at home in a vast selection of habitat types. These include tropical rainforest, arid scrub, swamps and mountainous regions. They can be found from sea-level to an altitude of 4,500 metres. As comparisons can be drawn between the jaguar and the tiger, so they can between the puma and the leopard. They both occupy a variety of habitat types, the puma also co-occurs with another large carnivore, the jaguar, as the leopard does with the tiger. Where the tiger has disappeared, the leopard has survived. The same is true for the puma. The jaguar has gone from the northern and southern extents of its range and the puma has become the dominant predator, though where they do both exist, the puma avoids contact with the more powerful jaguar.

Studies that have looked at the mortality levels of puma kits have found that they compare favourably with the survival rates of young big cats in Africa. Litters had a 72 per cent chance of making it to the age of 10 months, and young over the age of 10 months had a 92 per cent chance of making it to the age where they would be independent of their mothers, usually at 16 to 19 months. With African big cats the percentages were only 20 per cent to 50 per cent. This may be explained by the presence of other species of large to medium sized carnivores competing for the same food supply in the same area.

Though pumas are basically brown in colour with a white belly, the kits are born with spots like lion cubs and, as with lion cubs, these spots disappear in a few months. It was normally argued that the spotted coats aid

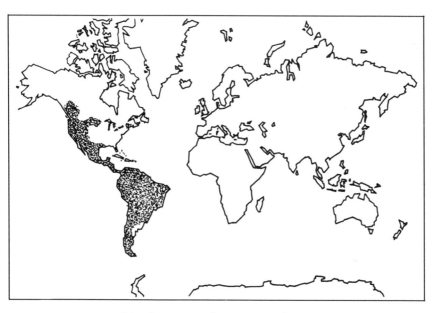

Distribution map for puma population.

in camouflaging the youngsters, but more recently it has been suggested that the spotted coats are a sign that their ancestors were spotted, and this is just a remnant of that coat pattern.

Breeding animals have fairly stable territories. A large male territory will encompass a number of smaller female territories. Individuals with no set 'turf' generally do not reproduce, as this would severely tax the available food supply. A puma needs to kill a large deer, its preferred prey, every ten days, whereas a female with young needs to kill one every seven days.

They mark their territories by scraping with their hind paws and leaving a deposit of urine or faeces. Spraying urine on rocks or vegetation does not appear to be a marking technique used as it is by the other big cats. On average there is one puma for every 50 square kilometres (20 sq. miles). It is further reckoned that if a population is to remain healthy, then between 50 and 500 pumas are needed. This means that an area of 2,500 to 25,000 square kilometres (950–9,500 sq. miles) is required to sustain that number of animals. (Yellowstone National Park, for example, is only 9,000 square kilometres.)

After a gestation period of ninety days, between one and four young are born. They will leave the mother before their second birthday and be able to breed at two but more normally three years old. Depending on the subspecies, they can grow up to 2.5 metres (8 ft) long and weigh as much as 45 kg (100 lb), though the females are about half the size of the males.

Pumas are not able to roar, but they can purr. The scream of a puma is distinctive to the species and should be connected with females in breeding condition. The nature of the vocalization caused early trappers to call the animal the mountain screamer.

When Cortes visited Montezuma's menagerie in 1519, he noted three species of big cats on display, one type of tiger (the jaguar) and two types of lion. One was the puma, the other was an animal that has only recently been studied by science, the onza. The onza resembles a puma in general size and colour except for being slim with longer legs, an American cheetah without the spots.

There were many stories of just such an animal, but they were dismissed as folk tales. In 1938, two brothers shot an animal that they claimed was neither a puma nor a jaguar. They had shot many examples of the two species so one would have thought that they would know the difference, but their story was ridiculed. In January 1986 a cat was shot on a ranch in the Sierra Madre in Western Mexico. The body was fortuitously frozen and later examined by three researchers of the onza 'myth'. They concluded that it was certainly different to any of the many puma specimens that they had examined. One of the notable differences was the presence of faint stripes on the inside of the fore-legs. Mutant, subspecies or a new species?

(OPPOSITE) *Like leopards, pumas can cope with a wide variety of habitats from mountainous areas to tropical rainforests, which gives them the widest range of any cat species north to south.*

(OVERLEAF, TOP) *All predators are opportunists when it comes to hunting, and will generally attempt to consume anything that they can catch. It is unlikely that these pumas will crack the tortoise's shell, though a jaguar would be powerful enough to get to the meat inside.*

(OVERLEAF, BELOW) *Black jaguars are not a different species or subspecies, just a colour mutation of their spotted counterparts.*

SAVING THE FLORIDA PUMA

The Florida puma (*Felis concolor coryi*) or cougar, as the species is commonly called in North America, is distinctive in a number of ways. The species was first sighted by European explorers in what is now Florida by John Hawkins in 1565. He told tales of 'lions and tigers' in the area. The lions were obviously pumas, but I'm not sure where the tigers came into it. The Florida subspecies is both the smallest and the rarest of the varieties of puma and a concerted effort is being made to ensure that this unique creature does not go the way of the passenger pigeon, once America's most plentiful bird species whose numbers were counted in the billions, but whose last individual died in 1914 at Cincinnati Zoo.

The Florida puma can be differentiated from other pumas in three ways: the tip of the tail curves 90° from the preceding vertebrae; there are flecks of white hair on the shoulders and neck and sometimes the back of the head, and there is a whorl of hair on the middle of the back. The whorl is oblong

The Florida subspecies of puma can be differentiated from other races by the severe kink in the end portion of the tail.

or tear-shaped and from 4 to 30 cm (1.5–12 inches) long. It is also present from birth and does not develop with age like the mane of a male lion.

These marks are important in distinguishing the Florida variety from the others as there have been a number of escaped or released 'pet' pumas in the area that are not of the same type. Pumas breed very readily in captivity and some unscrupulous breeders have sold young animals as pets, taking advantage of the United States' more liberal laws concerning the keeping of potentially dangerous animals as pets.

In March 1967, the US Department of the Interior officially listed the Florida puma as endangered. In July 1976, the US Fish and Wildlife Service appointed the Florida Panther Recovery Team to prepare and implement a plan to save the animal. The animal's former range had been throughout the south-eastern states, but was now confined to the southern tip of the state of Florida, in and around the Everglades. The plan's three main objectives were to: 1. Find and maintain any existing populations, 2. Educate the public concerning the animal, and 3. Re-establish animals in areas of their former range.

In 1976, a clearinghouse was established at the Florida Game and Fresh Water Fish Commission's Wildlife Research Laboratory to collate sightings of pumas and separate them into confirmed and unconfirmed sightings. To solicit information from the area's residents the search for data was covered widely in the media. By June 30th, 1983, 1,456 reports had been collected by the clearinghouse and of these 43 proved conclusive evidence of pumas, the remainder proved to be everything from domestic dogs to deer. Confirmed reports had to be a live or dead specimen, tracks, or photographs of animals or tracks. All but four of the confirmed reports were outside of the area south of Lake Okeechobee.

In February 1981, a capture programme was started to find out more about the lifestyle of the pumas in the area in and around the Big Cypress National Preserve. Two males were captured initially for the project. The cats were treed by dogs, which was the traditional method used by puma hunters, but instead of shooting the animals, they were knocked out with an anaesthetic dart. Each animal was tattooed in both ears for identification, weighed, measured and fitted with a radio-transmitter collar that had a theoretical lifespan of two years. The animal's movements would be monitored periodically from a light aircraft.

Dogs were once used to tree pumas that were being hunted; dogs are still used to tree the cats, but now so that they can be shot with an anaesthetic dart for study purposes as opposed to a bullet.

In January 1982 a further three males and two females were collared along with one of the first males, who was given a new collar. In 1983, three of the five animals from the previous year were refitted, but upon recapture, one of the females died when the dart punctured the femoral artery. The other female was not recaptured as she had a litter of kittens.

This study gave a much clearer idea of how much land a group of pumas needs to survive. The males had an average territory size of 301 square kilometres (116 sq. miles) and the females 194 square kilometres (75 sq. miles). An individual may travel as much as 30 kilometres (18 miles) in one night, or stay in the same area for a week or so.

One of the significant causes of death was being run over; in 1966/67 Route 84 was built which cuts right across the state. Known as Alligator Alley, in the period 1973 to 1987, eleven pumas were killed and two injured by cars or trucks. The state now intends to build underpasses for the pumas so that they need not dice with death on the tarmac.

One such injury victim was a male called 'Big Guy'. He was hit by a car in November 1984 and, due to the extent of his injuries, he was kept in captivity. He became part of a study conducted at the White Oaks Plantation, a private animal collection, under the guidance of the Florida Game and Fresh Water Fish Commission.

The commission imported two female Texan pumas (*Felis concolor stanleyana*), a similar variety to the Florida puma, to be mated by Big Guy and the hybrid offspring released in former Florida puma habitat to see if such a re-introduction would work. The released animals would be sterilized just in case they met up with and mated pure-bred animals.

Big Guy's performance did not indicate that he was aware of the importance of the project, as neither of the females got pregnant. In vitro fertilization was tried with sperm from a Florida male and two Texan males, and eggs from five Texan females. Neither of the recipient females carried the embryos full term.

Meanwhile, in June 1988 five Texan pumas were radio-collared and released in the Osceola National Forest, west of Jacksonville, and just south of the Georgia State line. The idea was to monitor their progress as a trial for a possible re-introduction with Florida animals. In March of 1989, a further two were released. The project was set to run for a year but was curtailed before the June 1989 deadline. One animal died of unknown causes, two were shot shortly after release, one died during recapture, and one was found asleep in a tree in a suburb of Jacksonville.

Opposition to the release project came from hunters and residents around the area. The hunters feared the competition for deer and the residents for their children's lives. A farmer across the state line in Georgia lost a goat every other week to one of the cats, but he was quite happy with the compensation that was paid.

Efforts are now concentrated on the study in South Florida and a captive breeding programme. It was proposed to limit the hunting season in Big Cypress National Preserve from 180 to 140 days. Numbers of hunters and kills would be limited and a closer watch kept on illegal doe hunting. In a study of sixty-four radio collared deer in the area, 15 per cent were killed by pumas, so competition from human hunters of deer is to be reduced.

The Ford Motor Company proposed building a test track in the Western Everglades. This spurred a study of the area as to its use by pumas. The findings indicated that the land was not used to any great degree by the animals, but the State and Federal governments did decide to buy between 50,000 and 100,000 hectares of the Everglades, 14,000 hectares of which is prime puma habitat.

The estimates of the Florida puma population range between twenty-five and fifty animals. As the species does breed easily in captivity I would strongly opt for a sound captive breeding programme. If they continue to monitor individuals closely, when a female has a litter, removing half the kittens might be possible: the wild is a tough place to bring up kids, and it is unlikely that they would all survive. By removing some of the kittens, the chances for the ones you left behind increase and the collection of wild stock for the captive project is not a drain on the wild population.

FADS AND FANCIES

Up until the mid-'seventies pumas were to be seen in virtually every zoological collection in the British Isles. By the late 'eighties there were very few to be found.

The *International Zoo Yearbook* has been published annually by the Zoological Society of London since 1960. For more than thirty years the yearbook has been the main source of information on the science of zoo biology, the art of maintaining wild animals in captivity. In the appendices of each volume are lists of species bred in the world's zoos, giving location, number of each sex and whether they survived.

If you look at volume 8, the breeding list covers the year 1966. It records twenty-three pumas born in seven British collections, not including animals born in other zoos that did not respond to the yearbook censuses or collections that did not breed the species, for whatever reason, that year. In volume 29, the breeding records covering 1987, only one zoo is listed as breeding pumas for the British Isles. It was not that the art of breeding pumas had been lost, it was just that by that time interest in keeping the species had waned and there was a drastically reduced 'market' for any surplus produced. Every now and again a species seems to lose favour with the zoo community and before you know it there aren't any about.

Pumas have a long captive history in our zoos. Major S. S. Flower published a book in 1929 that listed all the species of mammal that had been exhibited at the London Zoo from its opening in 1828 to 1927. It records the first puma the society received on June 3rd, 1828. It also mentions that thirty kittens were born at the zoo between 1831 and 1925.

The species was much later to be in the limelight as the world's first species of wild cat to be reproduced using artificial insemination. This was accomplished at the London Zoo where the kitten was born in 1980. She was sent to the Dublin Zoo in 1986.

The demise of the puma in our collections happened before the age of widespread co-ordinated breeding programmes. But, more to the point, the vast majority of the specimens held were of unknown origin, therefore useless to any hypothetical re-introduction project. Should there be a place for the puma in our zoological collections? There are two subspecies in danger of extinction, the Florida puma (*Felis concolor coryi*) and the Eastern puma (*Felis concolor cougar*), though I would imagine that the North American collections are best placed to deal with a rescue plan. It is surely better to use the capacity we have for keeping and breeding animals of conservation importance rather than merely exhibiting for the sake of it. When trying to expand the captive breeding programmes that are already running, like those for Siberian and Sumatran tigers, Persian leopards, snow leopards and cheetah, plus the more recent plans for clouded leopard and Indian lions, we have, as we saw on p. 24, the problem of existing animals of mixed ancestry that cannot be incorporated into the long-term projects for re-introduction. Our 'Heinz 57' version of the puma falls into this category. Surely a better use of valuable space is for other arboreal cats like the endangered clouded leopard or snow leopard?

Though the puma is fast losing its place in our zoos, it is important to note that it was one of the species that many zoos cut their teeth on when it came to developing the techniques necessary to breed and rear exotic felids in a captive situation. It is sometimes argued that zoos need to exhibit certain species that the public supposedly demands to see: elephant, sea lion, bear, zebra, etc, and the puma may be a little way down this list of popularity. If zoos are to be taken seriously as conservation institutions then a more enlightened attitude must be expected of the visitor and the zoo authorities in the choice of species in the collection and what criteria should be used in making the choice.

Like many of the big cats, snow leopards mark their territory by spraying urine against prominent features like rocky outcrops.

The Snow Leopard

Panthera uncia

The snow leopard is a species well adapted to life on a cold mountain slope. It has a tail that is nearly as long as its metre (3 ft)-long body to give it balance when moving at speed over rough terrain. It is covered in a thick smoky-grey coat and weighs around 60 kg (130 lb).

Snow leopards are found throughout the Himalayas, into eastern Pakistan and Afghanistan, and along the Chinese-Soviet border into western Mongolia.

Their main prey appears to be the species of wild goats and sheep that inhabit these mountainous zones, particularly the blue sheep. They seem to move with the herds of sheep throughout the year, being found at around 4,000 metres (13,000 ft) in the summer and at 1,200 metres (4,000 ft) in the winter. The problem is that as they and their prey are driven down the mountains by the snow, they end up in the local villagers' 'backyards', and both the cats and their natural prey are hunted by the humans in the area. As the herds of wild sheep diminish, the cats have no option but to prey on domestic livestock.

A humane form of leg snare proved to be the only way to catch snow leopards for radio collaring to allow the first proper field studies to be carried out.

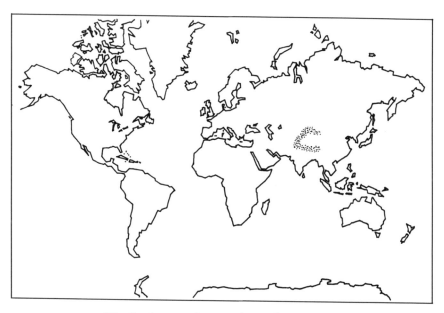

Distribution map for snow leopard population.

They are protected throughout their range, though much of that protection is merely on paper. During the war in Afghanistan, some Soviet troops acquired pelts. The Mongolian Government, after a rather suspect census, was considering allowing hunting of the cat via the purchase of a very pricy permit. The move was obviously aimed at the wealthy American and German hunting fraternities. India has recently anounced Project Snow Leopard, a similar programme to their Project Tiger, which has been the cause of some concern lately.

No accurate census has been made of the species due to the type of terrain it inhabits and what appears to be its naturally low population density. But it is probably safe to say that there are far fewer snow leopards than there used to be.

They mature at around three years old and are strictly seasonal in their breeding habits. One female at Howletts Zoo came on heat on the same date each year. Their cycle is timed so that the cubs are born in the spring as game becomes more plentiful. The gestation period is about ninety-five days and the cubs are born looking just like miniature adults.

Their vocal repertoire is very similar to clouded leopards. They cannot roar, but make high pitched yowling calls during the breeding season. They also greet each other with a prusten type call.

There are no accounts of a snow leopard attacking a human and they are generally quite timid if confronted.

Other than the odd individual, the history of the snow leopard in captivity does not really begin until this century. The first captive birth was in a circus beast wagon from a pair of animals that were both missing a hind foot, presumably from snares. The animals were owned by Hagenbeck, who, after mating was observed, moved their cage to a quieter area. The cubs were born with the male present and reared by the mother.

A snow leopard was received by London Zoo in 1891, but it was not until 1960 that the species was bred in this country at Whipsnade Zoo. Now many zoos are breeding them and the captive population is monitored by Leif Blomqvist of the Helsinki Zoo.

WHO'S ANTI-SOCIAL?

All the books say that lions are the only truly social cats. When individuals of other species have been seen to associate with each other, it has always been either a case of a courting pair or a female and her young.

However, recent observations in Ranthambhore Tiger Reserve indicate that male tigers there will associate with females and their cubs. Bathing in the same pool, sharing a kill, and mild play with the cubs has been seen. Soviet researchers have found signs in the snow of tigers travelling in groups of five to seven animals. There have also been reports of snow leopards hunting in pairs; one famous report is of a female clouded leopard being shot from a boat; when the hunters moved towards the shore the male attacked them as if in defence of the female.

Groups of male cheetahs will stay together for extended periods of time, though these groups are mainly made up of brothers.

So are big cats more sociable with each other than we know? Certainly in a zoo situation there are a number of cases where the pair has been kept together even when there are cubs. The only species, that I know of, where this has not been the case, is the puma, and that may be because nobody has tried.

When I first read of the tigers in Ranthambhore operating as family units, I was interested but not totally surprised. A number of zoos kept their tigers as families, though this is mainly practised in European zoos and the male is normally kept separate from the female and cubs for the first few weeks.

At Howletts Zoo, we took the practice a couple of steps further. The tigers had access to their large enclosures twenty-four hours a day, 365 days a year and there were at least two indoor shelters in different parts of each enclosure. When the female was ready to give birth, she would commandeer one of the indoor dens to give birth in and, depending on the pair of tigers, the male would be kept out by the female for between a couple of days to a couple of weeks.

Once the cubs were up and about, at about four weeks, there would be regular association with the adult males. One male in particular, Benghi, would actively initiate play with the cubs which, I imagine, gave the female a well earned break from the little striped gang.

Another pair of tigers, Jhelum and Putra, had a litter of four cubs on May 24th, 1981. In October of 1982, two of the cubs were shipped out to another zoo. In December of the same year the adult pair mated again. As the cubs were due in early April, it was decided to separate Putra off on her own and leave Jhelum with the two older cubs. The new litter of two duly arrived and when they were a month old, they and their mother swapped cages with the two cubs from the previous litter.

All was fine until September of that year when the youngsters managed to scale the fence into the enclosure housing the, by now, sub-adults. There was absolutely no problem, so we opened the slide between the two cages and ran all six animals together. The only time things got a bit hectic was when they were being fed. Not that there wasn't enough food, but sometimes more than one tiger would go for the same piece of meat, but after some roaring and shouting one would turn away and grab an unclaimed piece.

Clouded leopard males in captivity are notorious as killers of females, never mind cubs, though most of this is due to bad management. But three zoos have run the male with the female and cubs: Howletts with their first litter, Dresden in Germany, and Buffalo Zoo in New York State.

It is not a practice that I would advise due to the fact that there are so few places breeding the species with any regularity, and so what cubs are born need all the help they can get. In the case of the Howletts litter, all went well until the cubs were about six months old. At this point the male became very aggressive towards them and they had to be removed.

At London the male Indian leopard, Khan, was mixed with the female and cubs once the youngsters were old enough to go outside; and at Howletts the male Indian leopard was never separated from the female and young.

Snow leopards have been kept as family groups in a number of collections. The male was present during the birth of the first litter at Howletts. Likewise at Marwell Zoo, the pair Pavel and Vanda formed what appeared to be a strong bond, and, though they were separated initially for the birth of Vanda's first cub, all three were run together when the cub was about five weeks old.

Schaller's limited observations of wild snow leopards led him to believe that the sexes of the species may stay together as a mother with cubs would find hunting alone in the harsh mountain areas of central Asia, difficult for her and her cubs. The number of instances of 'happy' snow leopard families in captivity certainly lends credence to his theory.

A litter of cheetahs at Port Lympne in Kent were reared in the presence of the male, though I know of no other cases.

The pair of jaguars at the zoo in Belize are left together in the enclosure all of the time and no harm has come to the cubs from the male. Like the cheetahs at Port Lympne, I believe that this is a unique situation.

It may seem anthropomorphic, but when you work with big cats every day, you find pairs that do seem to thoroughly enjoy each other's company and greet each other 'warmly' after a period of separation for whatever reason. I would not dream of running a pair of cats together with their offspring if they were the kind of pair that grudgingly mates when the female is receptive, but does not associate at other times except in an aggressive manner.

It is dangerous to generalize with animals at the best of times and due to the lack of field data on many of the species discussed here, we are far from knowing all the answers. Captivity can alter behaviour, but what we are seeing in zoos with these animals is a complete deviation from the social norms we had thought prevailed; perhaps we are glimpsing something that for many of the big cats just hasn't been documented in their wild counterparts.

FIRST CATCH YOUR SNOW LEOPARD

If you are going to protect an animal like the snow leopard, you need to know what it eats, how many prey animals support a population, what is the size of an individual's territory, and what is the relationship with other members of its species in that region. None of this was known. The scant data that did exist was from chance sightings or hunter's stories.

The normal procedure these days to study animals in the wild is to put a radio collar on your study animal, then monitor its movements remotely. The use of modern tranquillizers fired remotely from a rifle allows for the safe handling of the animal to take measurements, blood and radio tag it. But you first must get within range of your quarry and that assumes you've found it.

The species has probably never had a very dense population. The rugged terrain coupled with prey species that do not congregate in large herds due to the sparse vegetation makes for a very difficult species to study. So the first photograph of a wild snow leopard was not taken until the early 1970s, when the eminent field biologist, George Schaller, was studying the wild sheep and goats of the Himalayas. It was normally Schaller's style to embark on a study of the top predator of an area: since the lives of predators and prey are closely entwined, one reveals much about the other. The snow leopard turned out to be an extremely elusive creature and Schaller was to get only a few hours' worth of observations of the cats.

Rodney Jackson and Gary Ahlborn started a four-year study in January of 1982 to try and uncover the secret life of the snow leopard. The study area was located in the Langu valley in West Nepal. The area was reported

(OPPOSITE, ABOVE) *The habitat of the snow leopard is the area above the tree line in the mountains of central Asia. Its thick coat and long bushy tail give it the protection it needs to deal with the extreme cold.*

(OPPOSITE, BELOW) *The clouded leopard has proved to be the most elusive of the big cats, and has thwarted any attempt to study the species in the field: in fact it has never been photographed in the wild state.*

(OVERLEAF, TOP) *Cheetahs may be world record sprinters, but if the chase continues longer than a few hundred metres, the cat will give up, exhausted.*

(OVERLEAF, BELOW) *Like all cats, leopards spend a proportion of every day cleaning and grooming themselves.*

to have a dense population of snow leopards with no human habitation in the region. The technique used to catch the cats was wire cable snares. They were placed along trails used by the animals and checked daily. Twenty-three cats were caught, after 3,899 attempts, but thirteen animals escaped the snares before they could be chemically immobilized. Not an easy subject to study.

If a lion is given ample time to become familar with the box it will travel in, the journey to another zoo will be far less stressful for the animal, as the box has become part of his territory.

Catching up a big cat in a zoo situation presents its own difficulties, whether the reason is a veterinary examination or moving the animal to another enclosure or zoo.

In the days before immobilizing drugs, it was all a bit rough and ready and not much fun for the animal or staff. A box would be placed securely against a door to the animal's cage, ideally a door that the animal was used to going through. For example, one that led from the indoor cage to the outside enclosure or a connecting door between two cages. It was common practice to scare the cat into the box with much shouting and the use of a jet of water from a hose. The animal would be eventually secured in the box, frightened and wet.

At the zoo we still box the cats on occasion without the use of drugs, but the approach is a little different. Boxes for big cats are slightly longer than the animal, slightly taller, and slightly wider. The reason is that if a cat does panic, it doesn't have room to thrash around and possibly injure itself. The box will have a vertical sliding door at one or both ends.

About a week prior to the proposed moving date the box is positioned so that the cat has free access to it. The idea is that as the animal's scent permeates the box, when it is caught the animal is in an olfactorally familiar environment. To accelerate the familiarization process, the cat's meat is placed further in the box each day, so that by the end of the exercise, the box has become a positive aspect of the cat's world.

Come the day of the move, the animal will be fed a piece of meat in the box, as per usual, but this time the sliding door will be lowered down behind it, taking care not to catch its tail. The box then gets loaded on to the vehicle with a minimum of noise and fuss.

Big cats are not normally fed on a journey since it is unlikely that they will eat due to the stress of travel. Depending on the length of the journey and the temperature, they should be offered water.

At London, we recently had call to move a male lion, called Pagan, to another collection. We followed the above procedure to the letter, so that when the day came, Pagan would enter his travelling box quickly and calmly.

Unfortunately, though the box was long enough for him, when the meat was placed inside, he would just stretch out and grab it, with his hind-quarters still outside the box. To get round this, we lowered the door to the box a bit each day, so that eventually Pagan had to dip under the door to get the food and after a while he would stay in the box to eat even though the door was still partially open.

On the day he was due to go, we fed him as usual, but this time dropped the slide down. He was so calm about the operation that he continued to

eat, oblivious to the shut door or the noises of us locking the slide in the closed position with bolts.

Where possible, I prefer not to use drugs when moving a cat due to the fact that it must be very disorientating to wake up in a very small strange place, and there is always the chance, albeit small, that complications could result from the drug. We do, of course, use drugs to immobilize an animal for veterinary reasons, to stitch a wound or for dental work to be carried out. Either the cat is hand injected whilst in a squeeze cage, or a drug filled dart is fired from a blowpipe.

Contrary to television documentaries, the drugs used to knock an animal out take about twenty minutes to work properly. If you go in too soon and move the animal, it can wake up, which is a bit disconcerting if you are hanging on to its head.

At one zoo where I worked, we were moving an adult male tiger. He had been darted and appeared to be out cold. As the box he was being transported in only opened at one end, and he was a big animal that took some shifting, I climbed over the top of him, in the box, to try and lift his head into a more comfortable position. At that point he stood up, pinning me to the roof of the crate. I could neither breathe nor move. Luckily, he only woke up for a few seconds, but I discovered that Einstein was right, and that time could slow down.

A rare chance encounter with a wild clouded leopard caught in the headlights of a jeep on a logging track in Borneo.

The Clouded Leopard

Neofelis nebulosa

The vast majority of what is known about this cat has been gleaned from captive animals. In my opinion, it is the most beautifully marked of all the cats. The coat pattern is made up of irregular large blotches of black on a brown to yellow background, giving them unusually large 'tabby' markings.

The clouded leopard has a body length of about 1 metre (3 ft) plus a tail of almost equal length. A male will weigh in the region of 20 kg (45 lb) with the females coming in at about 10 kg (22 lb).

The species occurred throughout southern Asia from western Nepal, east through all the countries south of the Himalayas, southern China down through the Malaysian peninsula, and the islands of Hainan, Taiwan, Borneo and Sumatra. At present there are no accurate assessments of its status in any of these areas, except from chance sightings and illegal stocks of local fur shops and animal dealers.

The species was first described to science by Sir Stamford Raffles, the founder of the Zoological Society of London, from his collections of Sumatran fauna. He did not give it a scientific name so its description is credited to Griffith in 1821 who dubbed it *Felis nebulosa*. It was given a new genus, *Neofelis*, in 1867 by Gray, because it was found to have a

At over 4 cm long, the canines of the clouded leopard are the largest of any cat in relation to body size.

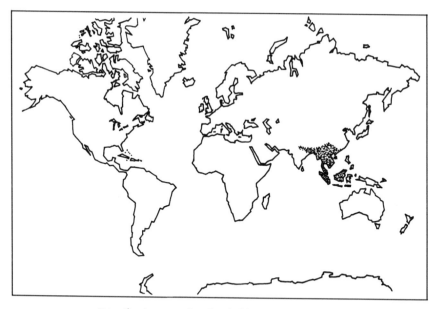

Distribution map for clouded leopard population.

relatively longer skull in comparison with other members of the cat family.

The animal has the longest canines in relation to its body size of any cat. This has led to it being mistakenly compared with the extinct sabre-toothed cats. The clouded leopard's canines have no cutting edge and the lower canines almost match the upper set in contrast to the so called sabre-toothed tiger.

The species is supposed to be found in the dense forests of its range, though recent sightings in Nepal in the more open deciduous tropical forests indicate that it may be less fussy in its choice of habitat than was previously thought. In 1988, an American biologist counted at least forty clouded leopard skins in the tourist shops of Kathmandu. Nepal is a signatory of the Convention on Trade in Endangered Species (CITES).

Four subspecies have been described, albeit from few specimens. The subspecies, *brachyurus*, from Taiwan is alleged to have a shorter tail, but as this variety may well be extinct, we may never know whether this is a general characteristic of this island race or just an anomaly of the specimen that was originally examined.

In Guggisberg's definitive text, *Wild Cats of the World*, he mentions the local rumours of a clouded-leopard-sized animal on the island of Iriomote. The Iriomote cat was not known to science until 1967 and it is about the size of a domestic cat. The native inhabitants differentiate between the smaller known cat and a larger animal that they describe as about the size of a clouded leopard. The island is also within the range of the species as it is only 150 km east of Taiwan.

There are conflicting reports about whether it is mainly arboreal or not. From my experience, in captivity it is the most adept climber of the cats and I have seen an animal hanging by the claws of one hind paw and swatting its cage mate as she went passed. Their ability to 'run' along branches certainly leads me to believe that they could well prey upon birds and monkeys in the wild.

They are sexually mature from the age of eighteen months, and ninety-one days after mating give birth to between one and three cubs. They were first successfully bred in captivity at the Frankfurt Zoo in 1963. Their maximum lifespan has been recorded at seventeen years.

DEADLY INTRODUCTIONS

The cheetah is called 'difficult' in captivity since a number of collections that have tried to breed them have failed due to the animals' complete lack of apparent interest in reproduction. This is, of course, not the animals' fault; the zoo is not providing them with the correct conditions for mating to take place.

With clouded leopards it is even more important that conditions should be exactly right because not only will they not mate but more than likely the male will try and kill the female.

Any time one puts two animals that have not been 'formally introduced' together in a zoo there is the possibility of problems. With cats, a prospective mate could be seen

Introducing unrelated adults cats in zoos has to be done gradually to allow them to become familiar with each other in safety. With clouded leopards, if they are not introduced at the right time the male will often try and kill the female.

purely as an invader of the resident's territory and so should be repelled, but the confines of the enclosure do not allow for complete escape so a fight can easily escalate to the point where one animal is seriously hurt or killed.

Introductions should be carried out very gradually with the two animals kept on either side of a barrier that allows them to see and, more importantly, smell each other whilst not entering the other animal's space. When the appropriate signals are seen – e.g. calling to each other, simultaneous rubbing against the partition, or both animals sleeping next to the dividing fence, then it is probably safe to run them together.

A male clouded leopard is almost twice the size of the female and so has a marked advantage in a fight, like a heavyweight boxer pitted against a lightweight. The size of the canines being up to 4.5 cm long doesn't help much either as they can puncture major organs with ease. Due to male cats holding the female's scruff in their teeth while they mate, it was thought that male clouded leopards killed the females because they were more vigorous in the mating bite. From an evolutionary point of view this does not make much sense as your genes don't get passed by a dead female.

With the other big cats there are field studies that help give indications of the wild lifestyle; it is possible to extrapolate from this to a captive situation and at least get some idea of the social make-up of the species and when and how best to approach an introduction. With clouded leopards we only have sporadic sightings of individuals in the wild so basically all that is known of the species is what has been learned in captivity.

We know that they occur in the tropical rainforests of south-east Asia; apart from that what information there is somewhat contradictory. Tropical species normally are sexually receptive throughout the year, but in captivity there appears to be a main breeding season in early December which would correspond with a birth season that occurs at the end of winter. When the cubs are old enough to start exploring outside the den at about four weeks old the weather is much more clement. This apparent ease with which a tropical species can adjust its physiological clock to a temperate zone system is nothing short of remarkable. I discovered this cycle change by consulting the clouded leopard studbook where all the information on births, deaths and locations of the captive stock is collected. By subtracting the gestation period for the species from the various birth dates, I ended up with all the mating dates. When these were all placed on a graph that showed the number of successful matings per month, December and January came out as the main months for mating. This is a good guide to the safest time of year to introduce your animals as a male will be more inclined to mate a sexually receptive female than to do her harm.

Feeding time can be another deli-

cate occasion for these animals; greed plays an important role in the lives of wild animals, as they don't necessarily know where their next meal may come from. In zoos of course a regular food supply is assured but this does not always negate an animal's inbuilt responses that help to ensure its survival in a hostile wild. This may explain why a pair that have been living quite happily together one day fight to the death.

Clouded leopards can be somewhat shy when it comes to exhibiting their normal behaviour in zoos, or, as Graham Law of Glasgow Zoo says, 'They are not 9 to 5 animals.' Much of what we are looking for in the way of indicators of breeding behaviour goes on after the zoo has closed and everyone has gone home.

For example, your pair of clouded leopards may be getting on fine but you have not seen any matings; they have possibly occurred, but you just haven't witnessed them. The female may show no obvious sign of imminent birth, so the animals are left together. The female may start to give birth but is trying to chase the male away as he has no role to play in the rearing of the cubs, in fact he may view them as potential meals. So once again you have a situation where the female could get killed defending the cubbing den or at best the male may just kill and eat the cubs.

A MEASURE OF RARITY

Alan Rabinowitz is probably best known in conservation circles for his study of the behaviour of jaguar in Belize in the 'seventies, and being instrumental in the establishment of the world's first jaguar preserve in the Cockscomb Basin in Belize. After the success of his jaguar project, Rabinowitz set out to conduct the first serious study of the clouded leopard. The study was to be based in Thailand, which up until then was considered the stronghold of the species. Animals are sometimes still offered for sale by unscrupulous zoos and animal dealers throughout Thailand.

Before the start of the study in Thailand, Rabinowitz visited Taiwan to determine if there was still evidence of the species. Because of a lack of time it was decided just to interview the people that stood the best chance of seeing the animal. Seventy forestry workers, hunters and villagers were interviewed. Thirty-three people reported having seen a clouded leopard, though in the majority of cases, the sighting was more than ten years previous. Most of the people he spoke to had only heard of the animal through hunters who had since died.

The last authenticated report was of a young animal caught in a hunter's snare in Nantawushan, Taiwan, August 1983. It is possible that the species still hangs on in Taiwan, but all the populations of larger mammals are declining, in fact the Formosan sika deer is extinct in the wild. Hunting and deforestation are carrying on apace; it is likely that if there are any left, they are living on borrowed time.

In Thailand, the aim was to collect data on the lifestyle of the clouded leopard, but as difficult as the jaguar was to trap and radio collar, the clouded leopard was to prove impossible. It could be neither trapped nor tracked. This may be because of its habits, but it may also be indicative of its rarity. Most books list the species as being arboreal, though many of the sightings place them on the ground, but as that is the level that people are normally at, then it is hardly surprising that that is where they are most 'commonly' seen.

The species, like the snow leopard, has never been a regular item on animal dealers' lists, which once again may mean that it is hard to catch or has never occurred in high densities. They are generally not good exhibit animals unless they have been hand-reared. My observations of the species in captivity indicate that they are nocturnal or at best crepuscular; whereas other nocturnal hunters, like leopard, will more often than not resort to a more diurnal activity pattern in a zoo, clouded leopards do not.

Though Rabinowitz did not succeed with a study of the species in Thailand, his time was not wasted as he collected data on Asiatic leopard,

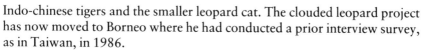

Indo-chinese tigers and the smaller leopard cat. The clouded leopard project has now moved to Borneo where he had conducted a prior interview survey, as in Taiwan, in 1986.

This indirect census had uncovered ninety first-hand accounts of the animal in Sabah, a quarter of which were from 1985. In Sarawak, seventy-one sightings were counted, 31 per cent also having been from 1985. More recently, in the summer of 1988, a friend of mine who was doing field work on gibbons in Sabah saw a clouded leopard run past the front of the vehicle she was in. The sighting was at night, but the animal was easily identifiable in the headlights. They waited some time to see if it would make another appearance, but to no avail. This sighting ties in with others, in that they appear to quite readily use logging trails for getting around, which is also the case with tigers in various parts of their range.

The clouded leopard is a difficult species to breed in captivity; since it is apparently so rare in the wild, it is imperative that efforts are made to augment the scant information that is presently available on the species. Due to their inclination to maintain 'wild' habits in captivity – even with individuals that are third or fourth generation captive-bred – they are likely candidates for a re-introduction programme; which is, after all, what it's supposed to be about.

Further reading

Bendiner, Robert, *The Fall of the Wild. The Rise of the Zoo* (E. P. Dutton, New York, 1981)

Bottriell, Lena Godsall, *King Cheetah, the Story of the Quest* (E. J. Brill, Leiden, 1987)

Denis, Armand, *Cats of the World* (Constable, London, 1964)

Eaton, Randall L., *The Cheetah. The Biology, Ecology and Behavior of an Endangered Species* (Van Nostrand Reinhold, New York, 1974)

Ewer, R. F., *The Carnivores* (Cornell University Press, Ithaca, 1973)

Gittleman, John L. (ed.), *Carnivore Behavior, Ecology and Evolution* (Chapman and Hall, London, 1989)

Guggisberg, C. A. W., *Wild Cats of the World* (David and Charles, London, 1975)

Jackson, Peter (ed.), 'Cat News' newsletter of the Cat Specialist Group of the IUCN. (World Conservation Centre, Gland, Switzerland, twice per year)

Kaufman, Les and Kenneth Mallory, *The Last Extinction* (MIT Press, London, 1986)

Kitchener, Andrew, *The Natural History of the Wild Cats* (Christopher Helm, London, 1991)

McBride, Chris, *The White Lions of Timbavati* (Paddington Press, London, 1977)

Miller, S. Douglas and Daniel D. Everett, *Cats of the World: Biology, Conservation and Management* (National Wildlife Federation, Washington D.C., 1986)

Neff, Nancy A., *The Big Cats. The Paintings of Guy Coheleach* (Abrams, New York, 1986)

Partridge, John (ed.), *Management Guidelines for Exotic Cats* (Association of British Wild Animal Keepers, Bristol, 1991)

Rabinowitz, Alan, *Jaguar* (Arbor House, New York, 1986)

Ricciuti, Edward R., *The Wild Cats* (Ridge Press, 1979)

Schaller, George B., *The Deer and the Tiger* (University of Chicago Press, Chicago, 1967)

Schaller, George B., *The Serengeti Lion* (University of Chicago Press, Chicago, 1972)

Seidensticker, John and Susan Lumpkin, *Great Cats* (Merehurst, London, 1991)

Tabor, Roger, *The Wildlife of the Domestic Cat* (Arrow Books, London, 1983)

Thapar, Valmik, *Tigers, the Secret Life* (Elm Tree Books, London, 1989)

Tilson, Ronald L. and Ulysses S. Seal (eds.), *Tigers of the World. The Biology, Management and Conservation of an Endangered Species* (Noyes Publications, New Jersey, 1987)

Tudge, Colin, *Last Animals at the Zoo* (Hutchinson Radius, London, 1991)

Turner, Dennis C. and Patrick Bateson (eds.), *The Domestic Cat, the Biology of its Behaviour* (Cambridge University Press, Cambridge, 1988)

Woodroffe, Gordon, *Wildlife Conservation and the Modern Zoo* (Saiga Books, Surrey, 1981)

Index

Numbers in bold refer to illustrations

If you have enjoyed this book, you might be interested to know about the other titles in our **World Wildlife** series, both £9.95 including postage and packing:

SEA OTTERS by John A. Love, with illustrations by the author

PARROTS by David Alderton, with illustrations by John Cox

You might also like to know about our other series on British Natural History:

BADGERS
by Michael Clark
with illustrations by the author

BATS
by Phil Richardson
with illustrations by Guy Troughton

DEER
by Norma Chapman
with illustrations by Diana E. Brown

EAGLES
by John A. Love
with illustrations by the author

FALCONS
by Andrew Village
will illustrations by Darren Rees

FROGS AND TOADS
by Trevor Beebee
with illustrations by Guy Troughton

GARDEN CREEPY-CRAWLIES
by Michael Chinery
with illustrations by Guy Troughton

HEDGEHOGS
by Pat Morris
with illustrations by Guy Troughton

OWLS
by Chris Mead
with illustrations by Guy Troughton

POND LIFE
by Trevor Beebee
with illustrations by Phil Egerton

RABBITS AND HARES
by Anne McBride
with illustrations by Guy Troughton

ROBINS
by Chris Mead
with illustrations by Kevin Baker

SEALS
by Sheila Anderson
with illustrations by Guy Troughton

SNAKES AND LIZARDS
by Tom Langton
with illustrations by Denys Ovenden

SQUIRRELS
by Jessica Holm
with illustrations by Guy Troughton

STOATS AND WEASELS
by Paddy Sleeman
with illustrations by Guy Troughton

URBAN FOXES
by Stephen Harris
with illustrations by Guy Troughton

WHALES
by Peter Evans
with illustrations by Euan Dunn

WILDCATS
by Mike Tomkies
with illustrations by Denys Ovenden

Each of these titles is £7.95 including postage and packing. Orders to: Whittet Books Ltd, 18 Anley Road, London W14 OBY. Tel. 071 603 1139. For a free catalogue, send s.a.e. to this address.